To Timothy —

Peace to all who
read this book. If one
Dad wanted you to have
this book.

Kathryn Muehlheausler

A King's Story

BY

KATHRYN MUEHLHEAUSLER

authorHOUSE®

AuthorHouse™
1663 Liberty Drive, Suite 200
Bloomington, IN 47403
www.authorhouse.com
Phone: 1-800-839-8640

First published by AuthorHouse 2/11/2008

ISBN: 978-1-4343-5555-3 (sc)

Library of Congress Control Number: 2008900215

Printed in the United States of America
Bloomington, Indiana

This book is printed on acid-free paper.

Acknowledgements

How blest have I been during the writing and publishing efforts of this book. I thank my son Bret for his support and research efforts; I thank Nick for his youthful exuberance, making his own meals, and his patience. I thank God that my prayers were answered.

A KING'S STORY

There were many other signs that Jesus worked...but, they are not recorded in this book.

John 20:30

Prologue

As dawn neared, moments before the Egyptian sun would cross the El Quisiya horizon, two thieves viewed a small family's campsite they had just stumbled across as they traveled north toward Cairo. A man garbed in brown was adjusting a donkey's harness, and the younger woman, with her back to the thieves, was playfully tousling her young child's dark hair as they shared a slight jest. The mother, dressed in dyed wool, with a blue mantle covering her dark hair, glanced up at the man, "Joseph, are we ready to leave?"

In a quiet, measured voice he responded, "Yes, Mary, almost ready. My Dear, I've been thinking about what we discussed last night--that maybe enough time has passed and we have traveled long enough." Loving eyes followed his son's movements, "We've been blessed indeed on this journey, and I think you're right that we've come far enough to be safe and should consider settling here."

The woman's answer reflected an obvious longing to put down roots, "It would be wonderful to stay in one place instead of moving from village to town and then on again weeks or months later. Son, did you hear? We're going to live here." Her son, however, was looking at the exact spot where the two thieves were hidden.

With the element of surprise rapidly vanishing, Hemar, in his usual abrupt manner and with little thought, charged forward drawing his short knife, "The kid's seen us, Dismas!" In a surly, rasping challenge to the family, he ordered, "Your money or we kill the boy!"

Moving as only a mother can when her child is in danger, the young woman grabbed her son, and drew him to her protectively.

Swearing aloud, Dismas followed his partner from their hiding spot, but directed his movements toward the muscular father who had quickly moved toward his wife and child. "Halt--"

Unaccountably, his command trailed into silence. Breaking into a sweat, Dismas stopped in total dismay as a wave of remorse overwhelmed him. Attempting to physically shake off the unfamiliar feeling, he menacingly moved his knife at the seemingly helpless family. The feeling of regret only intensified as he locked gazes with the beautiful woman enveloping the child safely in her arms. Her calm acceptance of the intrusion rattled the robber as her screams never would have. She spoke no word, and neither did Dismas who was tongue-tied for possibly the first time in his life. Hemar, too, was mute now as he looked to the younger Dismas for help. Moments passed—Mary simply held his gaze with the most compassionate look he had ever received. Backing up one step at a time, Dismas wanted to stay in her presence, but felt his intrusion was the blackest deed of his life.

Grabbing Hemar by the sleeve, Dismas skulked away into the vastness of the land.

Chapter 1

"Raheeb, faithful friend, I plan to journey afar again."

"Yes, my King, I know."

Gaspar chuckled at his servant Raheeb's matter-of-fact response, "You know?"

"Why else have you prepared your kingdom and your son for your absence?"

Instead of answering, the aged regent moved toward the open balcony and gazed west into the night sky as if seeking an answer amongst the gleaming stars above. Raheeb silently followed and as raptly as the other, stared intently westward.

Quietly the old man continued, "Truly, I must be a bad ruler to leave my people a second time. But indeed, I have weighed this decision for decades, Raheeb."

"Your son, the Prince, has ruled our lands for almost two years. Long ago the people accepted your decree that he take your place, though I am certain they cannot fathom what possessed you to step aside."

"Can you?"

Scanning the starlit expanse, Raheeb stated, "You must return to see if the man has fulfilled the child's destiny."

With a passion surprising in one so old, Gaspar declared, "Years before you and I began our journey, which ended in Bethlehem, I charted the stars. I have wondered all these years what became of the child and his family. Continuing to study the ancient writings, I am torn to pieces! My love for my country, my son, my need to seek again the child--now a man, whom the star drew us to so long ago!"

The words hung in the air between the two old men. Raheeb finally spoke in a low voice, "He will be thirty-three years old at his next birthday--a few months from now."

"Yes, yes, my point exactly! A man--ready to come into his kingdom if the stars and ancient writings have foretold correctly. My continued studies of the skies, the prophesies, the evidence of my own eyes, the experiences of the journey to Palestine, the warnings about Herod-- the source still so unfathomable after all these years–all point compellingly to a Master of men!"

Raheeb responded deliberately, "The portentous events proclaimed by the stars would seem to be near at hand—if not fulfilled already."

Gripping the balcony railing, Gaspar enthusiastically continued, "Let us consider the evidence again, Raheeb. He was born in a Roman province, and according to their astrological signs, his birth was a phenomenon." Gaspar paused to rationally present the highlights of the historical and astrological evidence. His confidant, smiling in the dark, prepared again to hear Gaspar's defense of the hypothesis that was also an affirmation of the old man's life-long search for knowledge—the hallmark of a magi.

"Jupiter and Saturn aligned together, then Mars the next year--surely when the skies bring such signs, we lowly men must consider what they foretell. Almighty Jupiter--to the Romans, their god who rules over all other gods and men as well! Saturn--tradition amongst the Latins associates it with justice! Mighty Mars! In truth, what else can be construed by this tripartite conjunction of the stars themselves, but that the greatest ruler of all times--powerful yet just, is near at hand!

"In the years since my return from our journey west, I have come to know that these signs were apparent only in the constellation Pisces. Pisces--the writings relate it to the Hebrews. Raheeb, the Hebrews!"

"Yes, Sire. Our journey indeed did end at the birth site of a Hebrew child."

As if this pronouncement ended the one-sided defense, the King halted and both men raptly gazed outward, each seeing again the wondrous triumph of starlit sights that had stirred their youth and changed each forever.

Neither man was aware of the passage of time as their memories journeyed back through the years, but after the crescent moon had edged slowly westward, Gaspar broke the companionable silence and Raheeb respectfully listened anew, "Does the world need such a king? Who but a powerful ruler could ever hope to overthrow the Roman Empire? Its talons ensnare the earth, grasping everything and everyone. That Empire covets the world! Worse yet, visitors to our land tell of a Rome descending into debauchery as Emperor Tiberius broods in suspicion that all are his enemies save a select few.

"Consider also that this same Roman Empire arrogantly rules the Hebrews as it does the rest of its lands, demanding obedience and holding its crushed victims in contempt. The Hebrews, Raheeb, are a people whose religion for thousands of years has held that a great king will arise from its midst, a Messiah. My studies of the Hebraic writings again and again point to this figure and the Jewish prediction of his birth from the line of David. The child's parents, Mary and Joseph, were in Bethlehem for the Emperor Augustus Caesar's census registering in the town of their ancestor, King David. Is this not further proof that the stars led us truly to the birth of a person who will undoubtedly change the world and could overthrow the now corrupt Roman Empire?"

Raheeb felt no need to answer and simply returned Gaspar's steadfast look of triumph.

"Let us now look to our own writings. Zoroaster, our eastern teacher and prophet, five hundred years ago, predicted a new religion and a Messiah. It was thought for a time that the rise of the Macedonian, Alexander, three centuries ago, might have been the person Zoroaster preached about, but though Alexander's rise was wondrous, and he brought significant changes to the world, no new religion evolved.

"So why now, after all these years, do I feel the need to journey again to the land of the Hebrews? I have not simply been rambling, Dear Friend. Zoroaster was 33 when he completed his predictions. Alexander was 33 when he died. My thirty-third birthday occurred while we traveled. The Hebrew child, as you stated, will be 33 in a short while. His time to rule is near, I am certain.

"This talk of ages brings me to my own. I have been blessed with good health, past 60 though I am. Of we three kings who each individually studied the heavenly messages and felt compelled to learn the reasons for such wonders, I was the youngest. When we parted those many years ago, we each agreed to remain in contact through the years."

Raheeb broke his respectful silence for the first time, "I myself carried messages through the intervening years between you three seekers of knowledge.

"Melchior was an old man at the child's birth and Balthasar, your wonderful friend from Sheba, has not been heard from in years. The last we heard of him was more than six years ago when he sent word of his plans to return to the land of Judea. Never again have we heard from him, although our trackers brought information two years ago that marauding Bedouins seem to have attacked his camp near Petra."

Gaspar spoke with a new urgency, "Only I am able, of the three, to bear witness that his birth was foretold in the skies. There were others who came, of course, and sensed his greatness even though he dwelt in a lowly cave. Indeed, you and I have discussed our wonder that even the animals seemed to adore and honor him!

"But enough of dwelling in the past. As this thirty-third year of his life approaches, I have made plans for this journey, and today I have decided that the time to return is now. I informed my son after we supped."

Gaspar put his arm around his comrade's shoulder and confided, "I will tell you, dear Raheeb, that he like you seemed unsurprised. More to the point, he encouraged the journey. My plans are to leave before the next full moon wanes. I will travel lightly knowing the land of my destination on this trip. I plan to take only two of the younger servants."

Abruptly, Gaspar felt the physical and emotional withdrawal of his long time servant--his friend. He continued, however, on what he had known would be a difficult aspect of his decision. "Don't be offended, Raheeb, I beg you. This is not easy for me.

"Your health has not been good for several years; this we both know. Last winter, it took all of our physicians and astrologers to keep you alive. You know my love for you is as strong as if you were my own brother! Was it not I who spooned your medicines to you when no one else could reach you in the darkness of your near-death? You have recovered, but are now in your seventh decade. As I plan to travel quickly, and the journey not an easy one, for your sake I must venture forth without you. Stay, friend, and be as astute an advisor to the Prince as you have been to me."

Raheeb, Gaspar's confidante, advisor, friend and servant, had known full well of the regent's activities and private preparations. He had realized that his enfeebled health would be a factor, and was prepared to convince his ruler to change his mind.

"Oh Wise One, ruler of these lands beyond what the eye can see, I beg leave to question your decision and to put forth my own humble plea."

"You will not change my mind, as I do this for your own good, rather than my own. I do not wish to leave these lands without you. It is my deep love for you which makes me want to see you alive again upon my return."

Raheeb now spoke with deliberateness, "Master, you have noted well as we conversed this evening that I was with you on that long ago journey. I served you in my youth as I do in our old age. I have obeyed your commands since before memory can recall.

"As I reminded you before, I served as a messenger between you, Melchior and Balthasar as you corresponded and continued your studies. Wanting always to assist you, I have made it my life's work to serve your needs. When you turned the kingdom over to your son, the Prince, I knew the time was nearing when you would want to go west again.

"How could you wonder that your beloved son and I know of your restlessness and desire to learn the destiny of the Hebrew child when always your first questions of travelers center on the lands where the star led us.

"In my hope of shortening our search, I long ago sent Zaphta, son of our old tracker Namon, to find news of the whereabouts of Mary, Joseph and their child Jesus."

Now it was Gaspar's turn to interrupt, "Ah, ever-practical Raheeb! As I searched the skies and the parchments, you searched the lands. You found them?"

"Sire, if we had searched in the early years, the trail might not have been so hard to follow. Treachery followed their path and we undoubtedly hold great responsibility for it."

Horrified, Gaspar queried, "How could this be?"

"You remember Herod the Great, King of Judea?

"How could one forget such a creature? Herod was all sincerity on the surface, but true to none, with the heart of a viper."

"Each of you three wise men, through what device none of you knew, received the same dream to return home by a different route and to have no further contact with Herod."

"They call us magi, learned men, but not one of us could satisfactorily explain the incredible occurrence of a night vision the same for each of us. Melchior told of his dream first. Balthasar and I were amazed to hear our own dream told by another. We thought if the child was protected by such powerful forces as could make three men have the same dream, then the child would not need our protection and would be safe from harm!"

"Remember the old rumors coming out of Palestine of the murders of innocent children, especially boys?"

"Yes, but they were so monstrous no one believed them to be true."

"Zaphta confirmed the story. Herod, furious at our not returning with news as he had requested, and fearful over our direct questions about a newborn king of the Jews, ordered his men to execute all male children up to two years of age."

"Our Jesus could not have met such an end," Gaspar stated unequivocally. "Somehow, I know he lives!"

"I too do not think he died then at Herod's hands, and as I had told Zaphta to search until he found this special family, he eventually discovered evidence of their joining a Jewish settlement in Egypt. The father was a carpenter, they had a son of the right age, and no one ever spoke ill of the family.

"Zaphta even heard a story about thieves who were near an Egyptian village named El Quisaya. The robbers had been in the area, and had the region terrorized. The story is told that the thieves left the area on the very day that the family came to the village. The robbers left behind all they had stolen from the people living there. Unaccountably, the credit for this was given to the family of the child Jesus.

"Further, Zaphta learned that one day the family simply left, and were not heard from again. He returned to me with no other news to report."

At the look of disappointment on Gaspar's face, Raheeb spoke again, "Zaphta came to me a few moons ago with news of a strange tale from the caravan drivers of a young rabbi from Nazareth who has been stirring up the crowds in and around Capernaum."

"Did he learn the man's name?"

"Jesus--and an Aramean driver joked that he was said to be the son of a carpenter."

In the silence following his words, Raheeb drew erect and with great dignity addressed Gaspar again, "You spoke of your need, your mission almost, to bear witness again to the truth that you three kings followed the stars to the birthplace of a new ruler. Think you that only you of royal birth were witnesses? I, too, was present! It was I who brought your gift of incense safely over the many leagues of our journey. The babe gazed upon me as he did upon you of higher lineage. Never have I spoken to you of my feelings and other events of that first night, but I will tell you now so that you may understand.

"I went back to the cave in the early morning hours before you awoke. His mother bade me bring the child to her. He looked into my eyes, but it was not an infant who gazed at me. Even now, I cannot describe the look or how I felt. But know this, Dear Master: As much as I love you, honor you, and have served you faithfully, if you would release me from your service, I would return to find Jesus and would serve him to the end of my strength and all my days."

At the conclusion of this speech, Raheeb began to kneel at the king's feet. Stung by the words and humbled beyond measure, Gaspar bent to raise the old man. "How selfish my thoughts to keep you safe here at home now seem, Raheeb. This day I release you from my service!"

At Raheeb's involuntary gasp, the old king continued, "But now, I beg you to accompany me to where the stars led us before."

Chapter 2

The crowd was a bubbling cauldron of emotion and noise and color as it surged the last miles toward Jerusalem's gates. Gaspar and Raheeb had become separated in the melee as the dirt road twisted up the hillside. Progress had been slow for several days as they had been caught in the great throng mostly composed of Jews traveling to the Holy City for the celebration of Passover. Yesterday had been the only day of recent progress since they had traveled on the Sabbath, the holy day when Jews did not generally journey.

Their trek across the sands guided by Zaphta had been uneventful, and now they were enjoying the present cacophony and kaleidoscope of excitement that surrounded them. Camel harness bells and the trill of children's laughter mingled with the no-less-jubilant voices of the adults eager to end their journey at the crown city of Jerusalem. The enthusiasm of their fellow travelers on the road, together with the inevitably slower pace, had actually helped make the final stage of their own entry to Jerusalem somewhat enjoyable since they could go no faster than the crowd itself. With Palestine abloom in vivid spring colors, they felt refreshed and eager to continue their search.

Astride his camel, Gaspar easily viewed what was the Valley of the Kedron miles ahead that would take them directly into Jerusalem. Turning in his saddle, he sighted Raheeb about a hundred paces back deeply engaged in conversation with a wayfarer also riding a dromedary.

Gaspar smiled as his mount loudly protested his request to allow Raheeb to catch up. He had little to do except guide the slow-moving camel and listen to the crowd's multitude of languages many of which he understood. Two Greek men on donkeys close by were discussing a strange incident.

"I tell you, I was there and never have I seen such events. Over five thousand of us had spent three days with The Master. We had followed him from the Sea of Galilee. On each of the three days, he made the crippled walk, cured the deformed, the blind, the mute! He did, truly! Daily he preached, telling us to live better, avoid hypocrisy, share our wealth. His voice, without effort, reached to the farthest edges of the crowd. The people seemed to hear his words without straining. By the third day towards the late afternoon, people were hungry--I know I was! The children especially were needing to be fed.

"Now this is exactly what happened, Euripides! A small boy came forward with a basket of loaves and a few fish and silently offered them to The Master. One of the men nearby told the boy to feed his friends with the little that was there.

"Instead, he took the small basket, said a prayer and looked upward. Then he told his close followers--they're called disciples--to pass the food among the people. All were fed and there were many leftovers!"

Euripedes' voice expressed his friendly skepticism, "You've never changed your story, but it is as unbelievable to me this time as when you first woke me up to tell me!"

"I swear by mighty Zeus that it happened as I have said!"

Greatly intrigued by the incredible tale and the person the Greek had referred to as "The Master," Gaspar wanted to hear more, but Raheeb was almost abreast and calling for his attention.

Clearly eager to make introductions, Raheeb brought his own camel and his companion's up beside Gaspar and spoke urgently, "King Gaspar, this is Sahran, an Edomite trader. I have learned much from him that I believe is important to our search."

"It will be an honor for me to tell you, Great Gaspar, but as I told Raheeb, I heard the tale from my sister who is known both for her exaggeration and her religious fervor."

"Let him hear what she said and judge for himself."

"Well, Your Majesty, in my travels I regularly stop at the home of my half-sister, Sarah, near Bethany which is where I am planning to stay this night. The last time I visited, she had an entertaining tale of horror or wonder--you decide which, after the tale is told."

The Edomite, clearly relishing the tale continued, "Dwelling in Bethany is a family of one brother and two sisters. The sisters, Mary and Martha, are as different as day from night. Well, to move us forward, the brother Lazarus is really the most important person."

Here Sahran paused, "Of course, if it is true, the most important person is the magician. By the way, as we have leagues to go in this accursed heat and traffic, do you want the long or short version?"

Raheeb interjected, "Please tell my master the magician's name."

"It's one that the high priests up there in Jerusalem don't want to hear any more about, I can tell you that!" Lowering his voice conspiratorially, he added, "The word is that they're out to get him and have a reward for anyone who brings them evidence of whatever new blasphemy he utters. He's got them jittery up in their big temple! I guess they're worried about the shekels I hear he's costing them."

"But his name please, Sahran."

"Oh, sure, didn't I say it yet? His name is Jesus."

Raheeb had been awaiting the look of excitement that Gaspar now shot him. "Listen, My Lord."

Feeling rushed to tell the story, the Edomite was offended, but Gaspar mollified him by asking, "Could you describe this Jesus to me?"

"Well, as to that, I've never seen him myself, but he is young, I hear. Or at least young compared to the graybeards in the synagogue who hate how he's raising the common folks' hopes."

"What hopes would those be?"

"He's all the talk from up by the Sea of Galilee to farther south than Beer-sheba. From your dress and voice, you seem to be Easterners, so you probably don't know much of the Jewish religion. You need to know that for thousands of years, the Hebrews–we call ourselves the Chosen of God--who, for the same thousands of years have been overcome and enslaved by whoever happens to be conquering the world at that particular time--well, we—at least those who believe strongly, that is—think that the Jews will be saved by a Messiah who will deliver all from bondage. Though I ask, what bondage? I'm doing okay.

"So, here comes this upstart Galilean, comes right into the synagogues, mind you, and tells all the elders and high priests that the scriptures are going to be fulfilled. Now this is hearsay again--heresy to them, of course. But they say, he said, when it was all said and done, that he was the one who had come to fulfill them! That is some of the blasphemy old Caiaphas wants to catch this Jesus saying!"

The throng of people had been creeping along at a veritable standstill. Their ebullient, conversationalist Sahran digressed, "Are they singing up ahead?"

Straining to hear, Raheeb started to answer that he wasn't sure, when Sahran began speaking again. "I guess they may as well sing! I'll be lucky to be near my sister's home by nightfall if this pace doesn't pick up soon. Which brings me back to the story, Raheeb here, wanted me to tell in the first place.

"Lazarus, he's the brother, remember, had just died. The family sent word to Jesus, who was supposedly their friend, but he had other things to do, or didn't get the message. For whatever reason, he didn't come. When he finally did arrive, Martha, the more boisterous sister, runs to meet him. The story I got from my sister was that she gave him a tongue thrashing, but then said she knew Jesus could ask his father for anything, and that if he'd been there, Lazarus wouldn't have died. Most of this does not make sense to me--what could Jesus or his Father do anyway? Lazarus had been dead for days.

"Right after that, the quiet sister Mary came, and the other mourners too. Jesus was crying along with them, but then wanted to be taken to the cave where Lazarus was buried. People in the crowd were getting mad at Jesus–probably for not coming sooner. Now this is where the story gets real creepy—the magic part.

"Jesus tells them to roll back the stone. Martha chews him out saying her brother would be smelling since he'd been dead four days."

Sahran paused and started rummaging in his saddlebag. Pulling out a tattered rag, he sheepishly continued, "The whole story is so crazy I wrote down what my sister swears he said. It makes the whole story better, I think, to hear the exact words: 'Have I not told you that if you believe, you will see the glory of God?'

"After these magic words, my sister said he told them to pull back the stone!"

The storyteller paused for effect, knowing from previous tellings that his listeners would soon ask, "What happened then?"

Raheeb, quietly urged, "Continue, Sahran."

"Jesus said, 'Lazarus, here! Come Out!' The dead man came out, his feet and hands bound with bands of linen and a cloth around his face! Jesus said to them, 'Unbind him, let him go free.'"

Gaspar made no comment, simply staring to his left.

Nettled, Sahran finally muttered aloud, "What's he staring at? The only thing out that way is Bethlehem."

Roused by the name of the small city and as if there had been no pause, Gaspar questioned, "Do you believe the story?"

"Bringing a dead man back to life? It was magic! I told you that all along."

"Did your sister believe it?"

"Didn't I say she's unreliable? She's a religious fanatic! Actually, she did believe it at first, but when I explained how it was probably a practical joke on someone, or that these particular Jews were in cahoots to make Jesus really seem like he might be the Messiah and have such powers, she saw the sense of what I was saying."

"Why did you write the words down?"

Uncomfortable with the old man's piercing eyes and questions, Sahran sought to end their meeting, "That means nothing. I told you--it makes a good story! The back way to Bethany is just to the left up ahead. I can't make any money moving at this pace! May your journey be a success and your burdens light." With these words, Sahran urged his camel forward.

As the curtain of people closed around the disappearing Edomite, the two old men were united in their silence. Gaspar finally queried in an old man's voice, "Have we come all this way for a magician?"

Raheeb slowly responded, "There have to be more than two people in Palestine named Jesus— it's the Greek version of the common enough Hebrew name, Joshua." Seeking a diversion, he noted, "Our garrulous friend at least seems to be right in that there is singing going on up ahead. Can you not hear it?"

"Only faintly, my hearing is not so good as it once was. I am happy that someone feels like singing today." Gaspar's words were in the querulous voice of an old man facing his diminishing capacities and the possibility of defeat. For the first time on this journey, Gaspar was feeling the immensity of the task he had undertaken.

"Do not despair yet! We were advised to make our way to the temple in Jerusalem to seek answers about the Messiah. On the morrow, we will have reached our destination. Zaphta already has our lodgings arranged for tonight. All will be well."

Needing to further express reassurance for both of them, Raheeb encouraged, "That Edomite is an undoubted cynic and talker. We did expect great deeds of the child-- the signs in the skies were for no common mortal."

"Raheeb, Raheeb! My thanks for your efforts, but think further. No mortal could bring a man back to life! If Sahran was right about the magic, we know that magicians are merely sleight-of-hand tricksters. Some are better than others, and this man must have been very good indeed. But a magician was not the person we have come such a distance to find.

"A great hoax by the sisters, brother, and this Jesus is certainly more believable. Power is a poisonous serpent. A child born into poverty would have little chance of overcoming a common background. How shameful it would be for all if this man has become someone's pawn."

"We have no evidence that this man is the same person the star brought us to. The man and woman, Mary and Joseph, were kind beyond measure. The child I held--so--never can I find the right words. He seemed to be almost--filled with goodness. Never will I believe such a thing could happen."

"He was a babe, Raheeb! We don't know what happened to him. Even if Zaphta was right in that the family went to Egypt, he could find no further trace of them. Both parents could have died. Maybe he was then raised by others who discovered his powers and took advantage of him."

"The person we seek is not a charlatan."

"Your words do give me hope, my friend. Well, listen now to another tale of wonder. Two Greeks near me were speaking about a person the one man referred to as 'The Master.' This man was said to be curing people of all manner of illnesses. He even fed a crowd larger than the one we are in now from a child's small basket of food. The Greek telling the tale protested strongly that he had seen all this happen with his own eyes. Now who knows if he was telling the truth, but at least these were acts of compassion. If we are only to find a magician, may he be someone with such goodness in his heart."

Faith in their mission somewhat restored, both men now became aware of the words of the song verse which had spread from the travelers up ahead. The Aramaic words were a continuous chant: "Blessed is he who comes as king in the name of the Lord! Peace in heaven and glory in the highest."

The crowd's demeanor was undergoing a change as well. Those not singing were in a frenzy, shouting, "The Messiah! The Messiah!"

"He rides in triumph to Jerusalem!"

"Long live the King!"

"Hosanna! Hosanna!"

"Deliver us!"

Palm trees along the side of the road were being stripped and the fronds passed among the travelers and singers. A procession of sorts seemed to have formed. One man, his face alive with excitement, reached high to thrust stalks into their hands shouting, "The Messiah--he goes to the Holy City! He leads us to glory!"

Chapter 3

One thousand years earlier, Solomon's reign had been the glory of Israel. His choice of Jerusalem as the site for the construction of the temple elevated her above all other cities. Consisting of pylons, courts and a naos leading to the Holy of Holies that housed the Ark of the Covenant, the temple of Solomon was a monumental structure of the ancient, often nomadic, Hebrews.

During the forty-year reign of Herod the Great, Jerusalem architecturally was rejuvenated and enhanced as she had not been since the time of Solomon. In another city, not Jerusalem, the magnificent Herod Palace in the northern part of the town, would have been the focal point of all eyes. In this city, it was one of several splendid structures that included three great towers known as Phasael, Hippicus and Mariamne. There was a great fortress, Antonia, at the temple enclosure. The greatest ornament to the city, however, was the temple itself, which after fifty-three years of additions, was still being improved by Herod Antipas, the current King of Judea.

The ornate temple was the heart of the Holy City. For a Jew to remain in a state of holiness, he must offer ritual blood sacrifices in the Jerusalem temple at least once in his life. Out of the ancient holy practices from the time of Abraham, Isaac and Moses, a thriving industry had emerged. Within the sacred portals, faithful families paid homage and supported their priests and religion. Turtledoves, spotless kid goats, downy sheep and burly oxen loudly awaited their fates. Coos, squawks, bleats, and baas raucously blended with sellers' chants. Clinking coins, dearly earned, purchased passage to a higher life as sestertius and denarii increased the temple treasury and monies from distant lands were converted into Judean coinage.

The overt sights, sounds and smells of the Hebraic religion were not readily apparent to the three Easterners staring upward at the massive stone, timber and metal structure.

"Only once before have I felt this overwhelmed," Gaspar voiced his thoughts.

"It rises to the clouds," breathed Raheeb.

Zaphta stated, "It is a fitting tribute to a great religion."

"Come, let us ascend," urged Gaspar.

Several hundred steps later, the trio stood outside the main temple pylon. Before they entered, they paused to view the Holy City below.

An obsequious bystander, after noting their foreign attire, inched forward, first looking around as if someone might be watching. "For a shekel, I will tell you of the rich history of Jerusalem and will graciously point out the grandeur surrounding our Holy City. Do you know which height is Mt. Tabor?" Glibly, he urged, "For a few coins more, you can hear of the many miracles performed here. I can take you to the Sheep Pool where recently a man who couldn't walk for almost forty years was healed!"

Lowering his voice, and again scanning the area, he bartered, "Have you heard yet of the scandal which took place here just yesterday?"

Raheeb, wiping the sheen of sweat shining on his forehead from the labored climb, ordered, "Be off! This is King Gaspar you are insulting."

"A King! Generous High One! It would be my most special pleasure to inform you of the outrageous acts of the upstart Galilean."

Again Raheeb had been about to warn off the man, but the latter's groveling words caused him to change his mind. "What Galilean?"

Sensing the chance for income, but careful not to offend the king, the tale-bearer sought a middle course, "The desecration happened yesterday in the inner temple."

"Tell us," Zaphta ordered.

Tossing a coin to the man as he moved forward, Gaspar took over, "Inside someone of authority will assist us."

The contrast between the brilliant Palestinian sun and the darkened recess of the interior chambers of the temple temporarily blinded the visitors. As their eyes adjusted to the dimness, they were aware of the approach of a silent black-garbed figure. Slightly past middle age, his robes proclaimed him to be a high-ranking temple dignitary. Bowing low before Gaspar, he spoke, "Welcome, King Gaspar, to the Jerusalem Temple. I am Jeroboam, a servant of Yahweh. If you will permit, it would be my great honor to attend you today."

Rather than question how a secluded priest would know his name, Gaspar graciously acknowledged the introduction, "We arrived in your city yesterday at sunset. Raheeb, my old friend, and I are no longer as young as Zaphta, our guide, so we retired early and arose late. We have made this magnificent temple our first stop."

A slight inclination of Jeroboam's body acknowledged the merit of this remark. "I hope your night's rest at the Black Grape and Bed was pleasant."

Gaspar stiffened at this obvious second remark concerning his party's activities.

Aware that his objective had been achieved that the religious leaders were powers in the city, Jeroboam made a surface apology, "Visitors of your Highness' status usually stay at the Black Grape and Bed. Also, word of an Eastern magi visiting our city was brought to us by those who know that we would wish to honor you."

"I wanted no fanfare on this journey and, therefore, have chosen to travel in relative anonymity. My search is for knowledge rather than recognition."

"How may we enlighten you, Learned One?"

Gaspar could not help but feel that the temple leaders had known of his mission and whereabouts for weeks. Gaspar and his companions had not attempted to disguise their purpose and had openly questioned others on their journey about information on the Messiah specifically and anyone proclaiming such a destiny to be theirs. Recalling Sahran's words from yesterday that the elders of the temple were seeking evidence against the young Galilean whom they had learned last night was the person in whose procession they had seemingly entered the city, Gaspar wondered if he were in a place of peace or enmity.

Testing Jeroboam, Gaspar ventured, "We arrived with a festive group of travelers yesterday."

"Ah, yes, as you probably know this is the season of Passover when Jews purify themselves. Although a time of great solemnity, it also is a time when families and friends who see each other at no other time of the year, celebrate together."

"Apparently, it was more than this. We were a part of a procession it seems for one the people refer to as the Galilean, Jesus of Nazarath. We were unaware of his presence ahead of us as we traveled, but he must be an interesting person and we would like to know more of him."

Seeming to accept Gaspar's comments at face value, Jeroboam warned, "You do yourself no good to seek news of this imposter. The common people certainly have embraced him for the moment. In a few days, they'll undoubtedly turn from him and give their adoration to another."

"Why do you say this?"

"People are fickle. Today, your friend; tomorrow, your enemy--rejected."

"Why is this Galilean so popular?"

"He is no longer popular, I can assure you, good King Gaspar. But let us not dwell on this disreputable false teacher. Allow me to escort you through the temple. Then our High Priest Caiaphas would like to meet you. Presently he is involved in temple matters."

Moving with their guide to the edge of one of several pools in the vicinity, Gaspar probed, "Yes, I am anxious to see your great temple. Even as far away as my home, we know of its wonder. But you have intrigued me, Jeroboam.

You say the Galilean is no longer popular? What could have occurred between yesterday when a procession of leagues praised him in song and today?"

Gaspar had been aware for some minutes of activity in adjacent areas to where they stood. Indeed, Jeroboam almost seemed to be deliberately trying to keep Gaspar from viewing what seemed to be a major cleanup.

Realizing Gaspar would not be satisfied until he knew at least some of the Galilean's story, the rabbi gave in to the inevitable.

"The crowds have been swayed by his words. He seems to have been in the right place at the right time and cures have been credited to him. People see what they want to see and hope needs little enough to build on it seems. Rumors have been flying for months. They attribute all manner of feats to him. Indeed, it would be entertaining if not for the seriousness of his offenses."

"What offenses?"

"Inciting the mob for one."

"An unofficial procession?"

"Oh, there is more to this than a parade, I assure you."

Apparently deciding that Gaspar knew little to nothing about the Galilean, Jeroboam spoke of the concerns the Rabbis felt at the words and actions of the Jewish upstart.

"He entered Jerusalem yesterday afternoon, not long before you. He really had few followers since most were innocent travelers like you simply sharing the road with him and traveling at the same time."

His confidence building as if he was convincing himself of the truth of his comments, Jeroboam built a strong case against the Galilean.

"Several years ago we welcomed him to our midst when he first began his ministry. Anyone who seeks truth is welcome to preach and to enlighten us and in turn to be enlightened. His views were radical, however, and turned many against him through careless interpretations of the Scriptures. The son of a carpenter, he keeps low company associating with harlots and tax collectors."

Becoming impassioned with his diatribe, Jeroboam failed to note the visual exchange between the three visitors.

"Yesterday, he probably destroyed any credibility he had!"

"What did he do that was so terrible?"

"Arriving with a crowd of his followers, he decided to impress them with theatrics such as this temple has never seen. He upset the tables of the moneychangers, ranted and raved, and shouted words of pure blasphemy: 'My house will be called a house of prayer, but you have turned it into a robbers' den.'

"The High Priests meet even as we speak to discuss his fate. At the least, he will probably be banned from the temple."

"Aiee…" the low, half-strangled cry from Raheeb caught everyone's attention and halted the diatribe against Jesus. Gaspar, previously intent on Jeroboam's words, had failed to notice Raheeb's reaction to the harsh utterances. Grasping his old friend, he feared the worst. Raheeb was bathed in sweat and holding his left arm as if in pain. Conscience-stricken, Gaspar recalled Raheeb's labored ascent to the temple as the king assisted him to a nearby bench.

Offering a water-drenched cloth to cool him off, Zaphta urged, "Be still, Raheeb."

When Raheeb showed little signs of recovery, Jeroboam offered, "We can let him rest in a room down this corridor where it will be quiet for him. I will have some acolytes assist you in making him comfortable."

After several hours of obvious distress with no discernable improvement, Raheeb was to be conveyed to their hostel. His labored breathing at least indicated that he lived. Zaphta was out making the arrangements and the sick man was asleep. Gaspar had spent a short time in the permitted temple areas and had met some of the rabbis including Joseph of Arimathaea who had offered advice on Raheeb's treatment. Now Gaspar was waiting outside the room for Zaphta's imminent return so that Raheeb wouldn't be disturbed any more than necessary. The acolytes assigned to help were talking with two newcomers and their conversation was so intense that it attracted his attention.

"For my part, I think the Nazarene carried the day. His arguments left me dumbfounded that a man from such a lowly background could be so logical and know so much scripture."

"Mark, you heard more than we did since we were back here all afternoon. Why did they even let him speak after what he did in the temple yesterday?"

"With so many people here for the Passover and many of them seeming to support the young Rabbi, I think Caiaphas is listening to his father-in-law Annas, and is taking a wait-and-see attitude."

"More likely, Caiaphas wants to let him condemn himself with his own words. Those were devilish questions they posed him today."

"True, but he infuriated them when they asked him by whose authority he speaks and acts as he does."

"That's an answer I'd like to have heard! What did he say?"

"He was clever. He said something like he would ask them a question and if they answered it, then he would answer their question."

"He dared to say that to them?"

"Yes, and incredibly, they went along with it."

"What was his question?"

"You'd have loved it. Didn't you go out to the desert to hear John, the prophet, speak once or twice?"

"I did. He had some interesting ideas and if our times, as decadent as they are, could produce a prophet, I agree he was one. But what does John have to do with the question Jesus asked?"

"He asked if John's baptism came from heaven or from man. The scribes and chief priests went into a huddle and argued it out. He had them on that because if they said from heaven, then he could have asked why they refused to believe John. If they said from man, then the people would have turned on them because just like you, they held John in esteem and many also feel he was a real prophet. Finally the elders answered, 'We do not know.'"

"They'll hate him even more for having to say that in front of a crowd!"

"Wasn't there a rumor that John was related to Jesus?"

"Yes, and it is true. My Uncle Mark told me that John was Jesus' cousin."

Another acolyte exclaimed, "Just listen to what I heard when I brought a blanket for the sick man. He was calling the scribes and the Pharisees corrupt and hypocrites!"

"That has to have sealed his fate!"

"It was almost as if he wanted to anger them. His words showed little temperance although when I heard him speak once in Capernaum, when I was visiting my Mother, that was certainly what he preached then."

"Earlier, they had tried to trap him on the issue of paying taxes to Caesar."

"Then they could have had the Romans put him in jail. Well, did he get us out of paying taxes?"

"You said he was clever, did he outwit them on that one?"

"That was one of the times he called them hypocrites. It was as if he was aware of their malice, but was toying with them. Now these were his words, not mine: 'You hypocrites! Why do you set this trap for me? Let me see the money you pay the tax with.' They handed him a denarius, and he said, 'Whose head is this? Whose name?'

"They replied, 'Caesar's.' He finished them off then by saying, 'Very well, give back to Caesar what belongs to Caesar--and to God what belongs to God.'"

"I bet they didn't like that answer."

"It surprised them I think, because they backed off. Then Jesus went after them using parables. The words were a thin disguise. There was no doubt that he was aiming his barbs at the Pharisees, scribes and the chief priests. But some of the things he said troubled me."

"Why should any of it bother you, Mark?"

"Don't laugh at me, but if he is telling the elders they are not going to be saved and that they are hypocrites, does not that mean that he would think we are too?"

"What should you care what he thinks?"

"I do not, of course! But--when I heard him speak before, and even here today--well, his voice has such quiet authority. His eyes are so kind, so honest. He looks right at you when he speaks, almost as if he could see into--"

"See into what, Mark?"

After a moment's hesitation, Mark ruefully continued, "Pay no attention to me."

Jesting, one of the rabbinical students said, "We won't if you start to think this Jesus is the Messiah."

"Tell us a story that bothered you, Mark," one of the younger students seriously requested. Mark looked into the young man's eyes and seeing his own troubled concerns mirrored there, responded. "Jesus said a landowner planted a vineyard, leased it to tenants, then went abroad. At vintage time, he sent his servants to collect the produce due him. The tenants seized the servants, beat one, stoned one, and killed a third. More servants were sent, but were treated in the same way. The landowner finally sent his own son. The tenants killed him also. Jesus asked them, 'When the owner comes, what will he do?' They answered that he would bring the wretches to a wretched end and lease the vineyard to others who would deliver the produce to him when the season arrives. Then Jesus said to them, 'Have you never read in the scriptures: It was the stone rejected by the builders that became the keystone?'"

When none of the students spoke, Mark thoughtfully continued, "He told a parable about a wedding feast where a king invited special guests who chose not to come, going about other business they thought more important. Furious, the king told his servants to go to the crossroads and invite everyone they could find to the wedding, good and bad alike. The wedding hall was then filled with the guests. But one of the guests was there without a wedding garment, and the king said to throw him into the dark where there will be weeping and grinding of teeth. His last words bother me still. He said, 'For many are called, but few are chosen.'"

Gaspar desperately wanted to question the young men, especially the one named Mark who seemed almost convinced that Jesus the Galilean might be his people's long-awaited Messiah. The old king believed that his search must have ended. As he started to move toward them, however, he heard a moan of pain. Needing to attend Raheeb, Gaspar agonized over the low-voiced statements coming from the group.

"I saw one of his followers stay here in the temple after he left today. He seemed secretive."

"They're going to arrest Jesus."

"They'll do more than arrest him if Caiaphas has his way."

Chapter 4

The innkeeper lumbered over to where Gaspar sat in exhaustion. Abram smiled sympathetically as he poured more wine. "How is Raheeb today?" he inquired.

"His pain seems less now that he has been bled again. He is not moving as much; overall, he is listless. Your good wife Judith insisted that she wanted me to leave the room and eat here while he is sleeping."

"It is good to see you downstairs. If you don't take better care of yourself, you'll be lying on the pallet beside your friend."

"You are right, Abram. I appreciate your concern."

Attempting to mask his feelings, Abram bluffly responded, "One sick person in the inn is enough! None of us are as young as we once were! By the way, did Zaphta find the herbs needed for the medicine for Raheeb?"

"Not yet, and we fear they are not to be found outside Persia."

"What will you do?"

"Zaphta continues to search. If he is unsuccessful, he will leave within hours to return home and bring back the plants and dried herbs we need. Raheeb and I will stay here in your excellent hostel until either he is stronger or Zaphta returns with the medicines."

"Good King Gaspar, we will be honored by your patronage. Whatever my wife and staff can do to make your continued stay more comfortable will be done as soon as we know of your needs."

"Many thanks, Abram. It seems an eternity already since Raheeb became ill in the temple."

"Not so long. It was three days ago; today begins our feast of Passover."

"Then I must return to relieve your wife. She will have many preparations to make."

"No, stay. This is the day of Unleavened Bread. All will be ready at the time it is needed. Our ceremonial evening meals called Seders, which we'll celebrate tonight and tomorrow, the first two days of the festival, have special foods most of which she has prepared. The Paschal Lamb is being readied even now."

"Actually, Abram, there is something you could possibly find out for me."

"What do you need done?"

"When we were in the temple the day Raheeb fell ill, a young rabbi named Jesus was causing quite a stir. He was debating some issues with the Chief Priests. I have a special interest in finding him and wonder if there is any news of him?"

Abram's friendliness underwent an abrupt change, "I know nothing of the Galilean."

34

Noting the landlord's closed features, Gaspar gently prodded, "I did not say he was from Galilee, Abram."

Flustered, the man muttered, "You would do well to avoid contact with this man. He is dangerous."

"To whom is he dangerous?"

"He has many enemies."

Gaspar tried again, "Tell me what is happening. What have you heard?"

"The Rabbis have been talking--actually, arguing, for days. Messengers are constantly coming and going. There are rumors."

"What are the rumors, Abram?"

"It is not healthy to meddle in temple matters."

"Exactly what do they fear about this man?"

"Their world would end if his words were to come true."

"I don't understand."

"Everything he preaches is an affront to them. He challenges their authority, their teachings. He quotes the scriptures often, and they do not like to hear what he says."

"Have you heard him yourself?"

"Once I heard him speak, but he talks in riddles and I could not understand all that he was saying. He said, 'Listen, anyone who has ears!' Now I ask you this--he was speaking to hundreds. We all had ears. How could we hear without ears? So, who was he speaking to, if not to us?"

As tired as he was, Gaspar couldn't help but laugh. Abram's good spirits revived with Gaspar's smile, and he continued, "I heard that someone once asked him why he speaks to the people as he does. He answered, 'The reason I talk to them in parables is that they look without seeing and listen without hearing or understanding.'"

"Strange words, indeed."

"Well, I have been a stranger to my kitchen long enough."

Gaspar rose, "I must return to Raheeb also. Abram, if you hear any further news from the temple, please inform me immediately."

"I haven't changed your mind, I can see. Yes, I'll let you know anything I hear. You probably won't like the news if I read the signs of the times right."

"Majesty, wake up!"

"Abram?" The demanding voice of the landlord broke through Gaspar's restless sleep.

"My wife said I shouldn't wake you, but I know you will want to hear the news?"

"Is it Raheeb?"

"No, Sire, it is the Galilean we spoke of yesterday."

Alert at these words, Gaspar listened in total incredulity to Abram's startling news. "Last night at Gethsemane on the Mt. of Olives, Jesus was arrested. It was late, past midnight. He was taken to Annas' house."

"Do you know the charges? How could this happen?"

"I'm not sure exactly what they are holding him for, but the general charges concern blasphemy. His disciples tried to stop the soldiers. There was blood shed. The one called the Big Fisherman grabbed a sword and struck off a soldier's ear. The veterans who broke their fast here had a wild tale that Jesus healed their comrade on the spot. They also said that one of his own followers betrayed him for a bag of silver."

"Who would have done such a thing?"

"Judas Iscariot is the name they gave. He had Zealot leanings from what I heard."

"I must go and see what I can do."

"Majesty, you must not!"

"Nonsense, they can do me no harm. I am a king."

"I tell you it is not safe--your Jesus claims to be a king and look what they are doing to him."

"Can you watch Raheeb for me? Have your nephew come and help, I will pay him well to assist you and Judith while I am gone."

"We will take care of Raheeb, but it is foolish to make such powerful enemies."

"While I prepare, find someone who can take me to where Jesus is being held."

Within the hour, Gaspar had entered the courtyard at Annas' house. It was obvious that exceptional events had transpired even this early. Requesting to speak to Annas, Gaspar was told that he was not there. At Gaspar's insistence, the servant told him Annas was at the house of his son-in-law, Caiaphas. The two buildings were not far apart but Gaspar, feeling that time was of the essence, regretted the loss of even these few minutes.

Asking to be announced, he had to wait to hear the answer to his request as the piercing crows of a cock nearby kept him from hearing. When all was quiet, the servant repeated,

"High Priest Caiaphas is not available."

"I must speak to him."

"He is presiding over a meeting of the Sanhedrin."

"So early in the morning? What is the purpose of the session? Speak, man!"

The authority in the king's voice drew forth the reluctant answer, "The elders are questioning a false prophet."

"Tell them that King Gaspar requests to speak to the Sanhedrin immediately."

"No Gentile may speak when the council meets, Highness."

"I will wait here, then. I must have the opportunity to speak to Caiaphas."

"As you wish."

Almost an hour passed before Gaspar was finally admitted into Caiaphas' chambers. Peering intently at the powerful man, Gaspar was immediately aware that the man would be implacable. Despairing inwardly, the old man fell back on his own regal integrity knowing he was fighting for another man's life.

Caiaphas' demeanor made Gaspar uneasy although his words were gentle enough, "King Gaspar, my sincere apologies that you have had to come here for us to have the opportunity to meet. I was concerned when I learned of your servant's sudden illness in our temple. Although I had hoped to meet you, I felt you would not want me to disturb the efforts to revive your servant."

"Thank you for remembering so small a matter. Raheeb is recovering still. My business with you so early, however, is because I have heard disturbing talk of the arrest of the man known as Jesus of Galilee, sometimes also called simply the Nazarene."

"A matter of little import, Your Majesty. May I offer you refreshments?"

"The circumstances seem to indicate that this Jesus is of great importance."

Haughtily, Caiaphas responded, "These matters are religious in nature. But to satisfy your Royal Highness, I will tell you that the Sanhedrin Council questioned him about his disciples and his teachings."

"What problem could there be? It is my understanding that he openly spoke to the crowds. Did he not speak regularly in your temple?"

"The matter is now out of my jurisdiction."

"What do you mean?"

"The Romans are handling the case now."

"What? What have you done?"

At the alert movement of a servant who had been standing inside the door, Caiaphas signaled that there was no need to intercede. "King Gaspar, what is your interest in this man?"

Unintimidated, Gaspar proclaimed, "I have known him since he was a babe. There is no criminal action that he could have committed. I have waited long to speak to you on this matter, and now you tell me he is not even here?"

"Your pardon, King Gaspar, how could I have known of your interest in this low-born person?"

Not deigning to answer, Gaspar demanded, "Where have you taken him?"

"The Sanhedrin recommended he be sent for justice to Pontius Pilate, Roman Procurator of Judea. The Governor will decide his fate."

Turning his back on the High Priest, Gaspar left immediately.

During the trip to the Praetorium, Gaspar actually felt his hopes rise. He knew little of the man Pontius Pilate, but the charges were so vague, he felt Pilate would probably try to appease the Jews, but without doing excessive harm to Jesus himself. Too, the problem was a religious one, and he knew that the Romans rarely interfered in the religious matters of their conquered nations. Since the

Jews apparently didn't want to punish Jesus themselves, preferring for some reason to use the Romans as some sort of scapegoat, the plan would surely backfire.

The litter-bearers lowered him to the ground at the Praetorium. Advancing to the impressive door, he eagerly requested to see Pilate. Told he would have to wait, he urged that his business was supremely important. After an interminable wait, he was ushered into Pilate's presence. The August representative of the Roman Emperor was seated as Gaspar was ushered into the room.

"King Gaspar, I extend greetings and salutations on behalf of Emperor Tiberius. Welcome to Palestine!"

"Your gracious words, Governor Pilate, and the urgency of my coming to you this morning, encourage me to quickly come to the point of my business."

"What can we do for you?"

"I have just been told by the High Priest Caiaphas that the Sanhedrin has requested you to intercede in a dispute they have with the man known as Jesus of Nazareth. He is a person I have long taken an interest in, and I would take it as a personal favor to me, if you would recommend that he be released."

"I would not attempt to question why an Eastern ruler would have a long-time interest in a person I had thought was a carpenter's son. However, since your desire to have him released coincides with my own humor to set him free, I will speedily send you on your way. Since he is from Galilee, and as both a Jew and a Galilean falls under Herod's authority who is here in the city for the Passover, I sent him to Herod Antipas."

At the name Herod, Gaspar expelled a horrified cry. Pilate responded immediately, "What have I said to so disturb you?"

"Herod--that man, his family!"

"Yes, the Herods have been in power for years. As the ruling King of Judea, his justice is applicable here."

"Justice--the children, so long ago!"

"Pardon, King Gaspar, but I do not understand your meaning."

"I ramble to no purpose. May I impose on you to give me quick passage to Herod?"

"Of course!" Raising his voice he issued orders to immediately provide an escort.

Pilate himself walked Gaspar out of the chamber. Their passage was interrupted, however, by an imperative message from Pilate's wife. The woman bringing the request was dismissed with the reply that he would attend his wife when he could. As Pilate continued walking, he remarked off-handedly, "My wife has become greatly disturbed about a dream which has frightened her excessively. You are married, I presume, King Gaspar?"

"I have had no wife for many years."

Sighing, Pilate continued, "Since you have been married, you know that wives must be placated or life does not always run smoothly. Your escort awaits you already, and hopefully your mission will have success. I leave you to attend to this new crisis in my life."

Gaspar dreaded the confrontation with the vicious weakling Herod who had murdered at least one of his own sons and had beheaded Jesus' cousin, John. The story as related by his landlord Abram, and recalled now in all its horror, was that Herod's audacious stepdaughter Salome had pleased the salacious ruler with an exotic dance. He had promised her anything, up to half his kingdom, as reward for dancing. Her request for the head of the Baptist on a platter was granted in part because he had made the promise in front of so many of the leaders of Judea.

Upon arrival at Herod's current pleasure palace, Pilate's written introduction admitted Gaspar immediately. Assuming his most regal manner, he hoped it masked his horror at his first sight of Jesus since infancy.

With Herod's wife and step-daughter Salome out shopping the Jerusalem bazaars, the ruler had apparently welcomed the opportunity to meet and question Jesus who stood, hands bound, in the center of the room. Herod had been enjoying the entertainment afforded by the chief priests and scribes violently pressing their accusations and awaiting his pleasure. Hoping to see a miracle, or at least an amusing magic trick from the pretender, Herod's cup now overflowed with an Eastern Ruler requesting a boon of him!

Having no compunction about interrupting the proceedings, Herod greeted Gaspar effusively. "Your presence, Great One, both honors and delights us." Gesturing toward Jesus, he added, "Pilate's personal note informs us that you have an interest in this man?"

Proceeding cautiously with the mercurial Palestinian ruler, Gaspar humbled himself in hopes of elevating Herod's ego and thus helping save the life he sought, "Your reputation, Great Ruler, is well known. Being in the company of another Royal is exhilarating, King Herod. Surely it is a rare pleasure for us both."

Herod's preening indicated he was on the right path of flattery so he continued, "The fame of your court, the buildings you have constructed here in Jerusalem--all are known throughout the lands. I had to pay my respects to such a fabled king." Redirecting Herod's attention to the prisoner still standing bound, but now unblindfolded with downcast head, Gaspar pretended indifference to Jesus' plight, seeming to align his interest as one king to another, "So the Rabbis have come to try to get you to see things their way regarding this man from your district of Galilee?"

Now that a regal personage was seeking his company, Herod's interest in the prisoner was waning rapidly. At no time did he see eye-to-eye with the synagogue leaders who generally deplored his worldly and lascivious conduct. Furthermore, the prisoner had refused to utter a word in his defense. Herod was already heartily sick and tired of the whole business.

"I have questioned him at length. He refuses to say anything, and appears to be no threat."

Gaspar slyly commented, "For a man who is said to be a king, he certainly doesn't play the part well."

Herod looked slightly suspicious at this comment from a man who from Pilate's note might have seemed more sympathetic to the prisoner's situation. Unable to determine exactly what his fellow royal meant, he decided to see where the conversation would lead and, therefore, simply agreed, "No, there is nothing regal about him."

"He doesn't appear threatening as either you or I might appear in similar circumstances."

"He's been a bore actually--harmless in the extreme." Sulkily he added, "I'd hoped for a miracle or some magic."

Seizing the opening, Gaspar commented, "Perhaps if he could use his hands, he might be able to perform for you."

"Excellent idea! Unbind his hands." An idea having occurred, he ordered, "My purple cloak—have it brought immediately. Any magician—any king—needs to dress for the occasion!"

Immeasurably relieved at the less dangerous direction the proceedings were taking, Gaspar struggled inwardly at the humiliation Jesus would now undergo. His sense of outrage and pain was so strong that he almost forgot the character he had adopted in Herod's presence, "Give him some water. Please, someone!"

Herod laughed childishly, mistaking Gaspar's meaning, "Yes, magicians frequently use water for their tricks. Good idea, Gaspar."

The elders of the church were frowning at Herod's change of heart and seeming dismissal of their attempt to punish Jesus. Jeroboam, the only one of the temple contingent to have spoken previously to Gaspar, stepped forward, "Most mighty Kings, this man has dared to call himself the Son of God today before the Sanhedrin."

"Nonsense!" Herod interrupted.

"Gracious Herod," Jeroboam continued, "the words are written here exactly as he proclaimed when we asked him to tell us if he was the Christ: 'If I tell you, you will not believe me, and if I question you, you will not answer. But from now on, the Son of Man will be seated at the right hand of the Power of God.'

"We followed up his own words by specifically asking, 'So you are the Son of God then?' He answered thus: 'It is you who say I am.'"

Jeroboam paused. "We needed no other witnesses at this point. We had heard it from his own lips! The assembly then brought him before Pilate who has sent us on to you for justice!"

Petulant at the implied criticism in front of another royal, Herod sought a way to escape making a decision in the matter. Gaspar, feeling that Pilate was the more sympathetic of the two officials, urged Herod to send Jesus back to Pilate.

Herod, eager to escape possible humiliation, now enjoyed reprimanding the temple leaders. "This affair is not worth our effort. You make a mockery of the King of

Judea by bringing such a case to us. Be careful in future that you do not so waste our time again. Free him now or take him back to Pilate, as you wish."

Turning to Gaspar, Herod cordially invited him to share a mid-morning repast with him. Gaspar felt his presence would keep Herod from changing his mind and there was a legitimate concern that if the women returned, they might influence Herod. Believing that if the Hebrew hierarchy did not immediately release Jesus, then Pilate would order it when Jesus was returned to him, Gaspar agreed, forcing himself to endure Herod's company. He fervently hoped he could conceal his antipathy to Antipas throughout the meal.

Later than he would have liked and finally having used Raheeb as an excuse, Gaspar was on his way back to Pilate to find out if Jesus had been released. The litter abruptly came to a standstill as shouts of rage interrupted his thoughts. He could see that the Praetorium was still up ahead and he worried about the halt and the crowd's obvious anger.

Calling to his litter bearers to put him down, Gaspar wanted to assess the best way to proceed. Standing amid the crowd, he realized the bearers had thought they were dismissed, and his calls to them to return went unheard amongst the other voices. Now as he tried to push his way through the maddened throng, fear surged anew in him as the shouts of the crowd revealed its dangerous mood.

"The true Messiah wouldn't let them arrest him."

"The High Priests must be right."

"Crucify him!"

The hate in the last man's voice impelled the old man to continue to force his way through the crowd that had assembled outside the Praetorium. All of Palestine seemingly knew of the arrest and imprisonment of the Galilean.

A gasp from the crowd and pointing hands drew Gaspar's eyes upward. The balcony scene pierced his heart and his eyes locked on the man he had spent his life following. His aged eyes could not really see the face, but clearly he had been abused. The regal cloak was torn at places and dusty as if he had fallen or been shoved to the ground. His hands were disgracefully tied in front again. Exhaustion hung on the thin frame.

People in the crowd were demanding silence to hear the proceedings above. Pilate apparently wanted an audience for his final decision. His voice carried out to the gathering below. "What charge do you bring against this man?"

"If he were not a criminal, we should not be handing him over to you," a spokesperson for the Jewish officials responded.

"I have told you to take him yourselves, and try him by your own Law."

"We are not allowed to put a man to death."

The crowd responded with cheers, jeers or pleas.

A reverent voice beside Gaspar stated, "He said he would die according to the scriptures." The man closed his eyes in pain at his own words.

Pilate raised his hand for silence. His challenge to the prisoner rang out in the clear morning air. "Are you the king of the Jews?"

"'It is you who say it.'"

"Do you not hear the charges they have brought against you?"

To the Governor's amazement, Jesus offered no further reply to the charges. Pilate felt that jealousy and concern over the growing influence of the young rabbi was responsible for the mockery of a court he was being asked to oversee. The man's innocence was apparent and he had no desire to condemn him. Hoping to provide a solution where all could save face and the Jewish hierarchy could have effectively chastised and warned Jesus, Pilate now decided to fall back on a tradition at festival time.

After ordering that the notorious prisoner Barabbas be brought from his cell, Pilate addressed the crowd. "It is our tradition to release a prisoner for you, the people. Anyone you choose! Who do you want released: Barabbas, or Jesus who is called the Christ?"

The chief priests and elders had worked the crowd well. Their followers were in amongst the crowd persuading the people to call for the release of Barabbas and the execution of Jesus. At Pilate's words, they out-shouted Jesus' few friends who dared to give public support for him.

"Release Barabbas!"

"Crucify him!"

"Let him be crucified!"

Horrified, Pilate tried again, "Why? What harm has he done?"

The crowd became even more frenzied shouting their choice louder still. "Barabbas! Barabbas!"

Fearing a riot, he held his hands out for silence. His wife's frightening dream to have nothing to do with the Nazarene suddenly being recalled, he ordered that a nearby bowl of water be brought forward. Deliberately he washed his hands in front of the mob saying, "I am innocent of this man's blood. It is your concern."

Barabbas, as his shackles were unlocked, stared in disbelief at the figure being taken away at Pilate's orders to be scourged and crucified for him. The intense dark brown eyes of the man Pilate had just called the Christ would haunt him all the rest of the days, and particularly the nights, of his life.

Chapter 5

Insignificantly crushed in the crowd, Gaspar could not believe Pilate had just ordered the crucifixion of an innocent person. Visions of the cruelty to come brutalized the remembered tenderness of the birth he had witnessed at Bethlehem. The baby, the child, the man--destined to be nailed to the cross from birth! Who could stop this farce? Pilate would not; Herod was impotent; the Chief Priests seemed the manipulative power behind the whole of it. His eyes, rising to the vacant balcony where the injustice had been perpetrated, were drawn to the rapidly darkening skies. To his overwrought senses, it appeared even the heavens above were distraught at the events which had just transpired.

Wildly the old man looked for succor and support. Where were the thousands who had hung on the young teacher's words? The miracles performed had undoubtedly been witnessed by many of the same people who had made up the mob today. Where were those he had cured? His followers--those men called the disciples--could they not mount support? He knew none of their names. The Big Fisherman--where could he be found? What could a follower of Jesus with such a common street name do to gain support and sway officials who had determined their stance? More than likely, the disciples would be imprisoned and even put to death for attempting to intervene and supporting Jesus.

Not willing to concede defeat although feeling completely powerless, Gaspar tried to fight his way forward through the milling throng. His strength was nothing compared to the numbers against him. Giving in, he let himself be moved as the rabble willed.

The crack of a whip in an interior courtyard stilled the crowd. The scourging had begun. Again and again, the harsh slash of leather sounded against flesh. Monotonously, the whip ripped and shredded. Most in the crowd were silent, but somebody was calling aloud the count: "--nineteen, twenty...." The whip could be heard in an unholy syncopation: swish-slash, swish-slash. At thirty-nine the relentless count and the whip ceased--forty, less one, the allotted punishment for one not of Roman citizenship.

Body limp with sweat, and his spirit weakened as if he had endured the strokes himself, the old man was shoved back into a wall. Spent, he remained there, despairing of the will to live. Suddenly, someone shouted, "He comes!"

Soldiers unceremoniously shoved the spectators aside clearing a wide swath for the condemned man to tread toward Calvary. The old man was glad his position against the wall kept away the terrible sight of his beloved Jesus struggling to his death. The sounds alone were almost more than he could endure.

"Make way, or we'll have you carrying the crossbar as well!"

"He's covered in blood!"

"A crown of thorns for a king--that's rich!"

Slowly, the crowd dispersed. Some followed the weary way to Golgotha, also called the place of the skull. Others exulted. Some wanted only to slink away from the horror they had helped perpetrate. Many wept. The paradox for the faithful: Had God deserted them?

Gaspar, too, was torn. Could he endure witnessing the death of the gentle man bearing his cross up the hills of Jerusalem? He was with the babe at the beginning, must he not finish what he had seen begun? Or could Pilate yet be influenced to stay the sentence?

Deciding on the latter course, Gaspar moved toward the inner Praetorium, but found his clothes caught on a large thorn bush. Attempting to disentangle himself, his right hand was gouged by a steely barb. Instinctively reacting, he jerked, but then impaled the back of his hand on one of the nail-length thorns. The intense pain staggered him, and he almost fainted as he drew the thorn out half the width of his pierced hand. The deep wounds bled profusely, but he ignored them except to bind his hand with material torn from his clothing.

The courtyard was now completely empty, and he staggered forward in weariness and pain to try again to persuade Pilate to halt the proceedings. His worn and bloody appearance working against him, the guard contemptuously dismissed his request saying Pilate had given orders not to be disturbed and that no further official business would be conducted this day.

Realizing the uselessness of pursuing this course, Gaspar sorrowfully plodded in the wake of the last of those moving toward Golgotha. Mental and physical pain a part of him, he trudged toward the notorious place of the skull. At its base, he halted and looked upward. Three crosses etched against the skyline forced him to his knees. Dropping his head, he doubted he had the strength to continue. Despondently, he thought: I'll die here with the man I sought; maybe this is the fate defined for me.

"Old man, this is no place for you."

Startled from his stupor, he stared into the hardened eyes of a young man crouched nearby under the shade of a date palm tree. There was no compassion in the other's eyes, and Gaspar instinctively knew the man, who was hardly more than a youth, had been watching his slow, painful movements toward the hill of Golgotha and his fall of despair.

His only concern being Jesus, Gaspar had no energy to spare for the cruel jesting of one who had probably been in the mob calling for the crucifixion. Neither man moved nor directed a comment to the other for several minutes.

Shrewdly, the younger man bided his time. At length, the old man attempted to rise. Forgetful of his bandaged hand, he pushed upward with it. Pain shot through him anew and fresh blood oozed from the makeshift bandage as he collapsed back on the ground. Glancing swiftly up to the height, the man lounging in the shade waited, but offered no assistance.

Gaspar, as only a king might do, brought a leonine look to bear on the younger man. Insolently, the seemingly relaxed stranger shredded a leaf frond while eyeing the injured man.

Nodding toward the height above them, he finally asked, "Want to get to the top?"

Humiliated and feeling at the end of his strength, Gaspar felt every year of his great age. With his blood dripping onto the dusty road and no other aid in sight, he guardedly said, "My strength will return momentarily."

Eyeing again the crosses upon the hilltop, the lounger exhibited a sense of urgency he had masked before. Harshly he queried, "Why else would you be here if you didn't want to gawk at the condemned men?"

With years of experience in judging others, Gaspar assessed that the young man must need his help as much as Gaspar needed his. Some urgency required the younger to want to climb the height, but he was obviously reluctant to go alone. Reviewing the man's question about condemned men, Gaspar realized he was probably in the company of a criminal. He felt no fear for his personal safety, however, because as nonchalant as the man wanted to appear, Gaspar sensed that they shared a similar pain.

He knew his evaluation was close to the mark, when the other broke the silence, "Well, do you want to go up before they die or not?"

Mentally noting again the reference to more than one person, Gaspar quietly spoke, "Your assistance would be appreciated."

Betraying his background, the other questioned, "What's in it for me?"

"Getting to the top."

Startled that the old man was apparently sharper than he looked, the youth eyed him closer, then rose and strode over to Gaspar. None too gently, he assisted Gaspar to rise.

Although exhausted and in pain, Gaspar noted that the young man walked with a slight stiffness as if he was in physical pain too. Even though both men were impeded, they made progress at first. But Gaspar began to move slower and slower as Golgotha's steepness overwhelmed him, and his hand throbbed and continued oozing. Finally, in exasperation, his comrade said, "You're bleeding like a stuck goat!"

"Please, let me rest. You go ahead; we are almost near the top."

Eyes ahead where the three crosses pierced the skyline, the youth began to move away, but hesitated and returned, "Do you have something to re-bandage your hand?"

"Here, tear this more."

Even more roughly, the desperate man ripped off a new strip of cloth and wound it over the first bloody bandage. As he finished, he urged, "On your feet, old man!"

Nearing the zenith, Gaspar staggered as his anguished eyes looked upon Jesus, the Christ, in the last stages of his mortal life. His comrade hesitated also and uttered a snarl of ineffective rage as he too took in the scene of horror.

Grotesquely outlined against a near-black sky, the three wooden crosses bore suffering men. Two unknown criminals hung strapped to crosses--how long they had hung there Gaspar could not have determined. Upon the central cross hung the limp body of the man who had claimed to be the Son of God. Hands and arms had been nailed to the boards unlike the other two men. Rivulets of blood seeped from the circlet of thorns pressed into his head. The sides and shoulders of his thin body gave graphic evidence of the scourging he had endured. Gaspar prayed to he knew not whom that the closed eyes indicated death.

Fewer than thirty people occupied the stark hilltop. Soldiers diced at the foot of the middle cross; mourners were mostly alone, except for one group of weeping women and a young man hardly older than the youth whose body trembled by his side.

Observing the direction of his companion's haunted eyes, Gaspar quietly questioned, "Who is he?"

"My brother Dismas."

"I'm sorry." The words of sympathy somehow roused the wrath of the other.

"Don't be! This life is nothing to be sorry about leaving!" Angered beyond reason, he drew away from Gaspar as if the old man represented all the people and the events in his life which had conspired to place him here to view his dying brother.

Wanting to say more, Gaspar waited as the enraged younger brother walked slowly toward the far cross. Gaspar then was distracted as several of the temple rabbis who had previously climbed the hill, angrily spoke to the soldiers, "The inscription! Who authorized that sign? Take it down immediately!"

The soldiers ceased their dicing and the leader addressed the irate speaker, "We were told to hang this sign."

"It is wrong! Change it at once!"

"The King of the Jews," the soldier read in a perplexed voice. "What is wrong?"

"No! It was to read, "He said he was the King of the Jews.""

"He'll be dead in no time. It will come down then."

Furious, they moved away still gesturing and talking angrily about the inscription.

Humbly, Gaspar recalled the words Raheeb and he had spoken before they undertook their journey--they would be witnesses that the star of Bethlehem had led them to a child of destiny. The sign proclaimed him King just as the star had heralded a royal birth. He and Melchior and Balthasar had not been led astray!

The comfort was fleeting as he slowly found the courage to look again upon the pain-wracked body above him. That an innocent human being should have to endure this intense anguish! How could men do this to one another? As if his thoughts were known, Jesus spoke, "'Father, forgive them; they know not what they do.'"

Unaffected, a burly soldier approached as if offering water. Holding a sponge to the parched lips as the suffering man jerked away, he mocked, "Don't like vinegar, eh?"

Others jeered, "He saved others! If you are God's son, come down from the cross!"

"He is King of Israel! Come down from the cross now, and we will believe."

"Let God rescue him!"

Sorrowing, an onlooker turned to leave muttering, "He turned water into wine. Now he drinks vinegar and is jeered."

One of the criminals joined in the abuse. "'Are you not the Christ?'" he said. "'Save yourself and us as well.'"

The criminal who Gaspar now knew as Dismas rebuked the other, "'Have you no fear of God at all?'" he asked. "We have the same sentence as he does--but in our case we deserve it. We are paying for what we did. But this man has done nothing wrong. Dismas continued, "'Jesus, remember me when you come into your kingdom.'"

"'Indeed, I promise you,'" Jesus replied, "'today you will be with me in paradise.'"

Gaspar wondered what the angry young brother would think of these words from the dying man's lips. Looking around in the dim light, however, Gaspar could not see Dismas' brother. For himself, the wonder of the moment was that given Jesus' own agony, he was still concerned with others.

The soft sobs of several women drew Gaspar's attention. Peering closer, he recognized one of them as Mary, Jesus' mother. Though she was racked with misery, the purity and beauty that was both physical and spiritual had not palled through the years. The young man he had glimpsed earlier at the foot of the cross, held her close in comfort. Jesus finally spoke to them as they mourned, "'Woman, this is your son.'" Then to the man, "'This is your mother.'" The atrocities done to her son appeared to have almost literally pierced her heart, and at the words from Jesus, the young man held her tenderly. Gaspar backed away feeling he could not intrude on her sorrow.

Darkness seemed to have overcome the day, as the sun was eclipsed. The tortured, gaunt man cried out in a loud voice, "'Eloi, Eloi, lama sabachthani?'" The onlookers questioned why he called upon the Old Testament prophet Elijah, at such a time. Another despairingly interpreted, he has called out, "'My God, my God, why have you deserted me?'"

Breathing his last, Jesus uttered, "'Father, into your hands I commit my spirit.'"

At the moment of death, the heavens poured forth thunder and lightning. Torrents of rain pummeled the earth. Lightning, bright as day, flashed across the macabre scene. Gaspar, although drenched, remained with the others, awe-struck at the elemental display in the distance, as thunder and lightning centered over Jerusalem itself. A great thunderbolt apparently hit a building in the city as those on the hillside heard a reverberating shatter.

Gaspar bowed his head dispiritedly as the rain pelted him. Jesus was dead.

Agonizing, he tried to fathom why this had been allowed to happen. This man had suffered so intensely because he had told men to live better and to love one another. Some great entity had apparently granted Jesus special powers to heal the sick and to bring joy. It made no sense to the old man that a god who could control the heavens and bring people back to life would then let his own son die so cruelly by the hands of men. Abjectly, he mourned.

Since it was Preparation Day, the day before the solemn Sabbath, the Jews wanted the body of Jesus taken off the cross and buried. Wanting to have the grisly proceedings of the entire day over, the soldiers broke the legs of both criminals to hasten death. Although Jesus had already died, as a final precaution, one of the soldiers pierced his side with a lance. The last of his blood and water immediately flowed forth spattering the soldier.

Thunder and lightning flashed across the skies while rain drenched the few remaining mourners and soldiers. A Centurion standing near spoke from the heart, "This was a great and good man."

Wanting to believe in the man whom he had followed so loyally, Gaspar could only watch in resignation and defeat as the lifeless body was lowered into the mother's waiting arms. Her renewed tears as she held her child's mutilated body, and rocked him in death as before she had rocked him in life, were poignant reminders of the atrocities of the day. Gaspar felt overwhelmed, but moved forward to assist in any small way he could.

He stiffened in alarm as a man whom he recognized from the temple as Joseph of Arimathaea, a member of the Sanhedrin, approached. Mary, however, appeared to accept his presence. Devoutly attending upon the dead man, Joseph laid out a shroud, and whispered words of comfort to Mary, "Pilate has given me permission to bury the body."

With no intention other than to be present at the hurried burial, Gaspar followed respectfully in the wake of the mourners with a few other women. Jesus was laid in his wrappings in a tomb hewn from stone in which no one had yet been buried. Soldiers, who for reasons unknown to Gaspar, had been assigned to guard the tomb, shoved a gigantic stone in place to enclose the body in its final resting place.

Racked in mental and physical anguish, Gaspar turned to leave, when the young man who had been at the foot of the cross, addressed him, "Sir, I am John, a follower--a friend--of Jesus. His mother has requested to speak to you. Will you come to her?"

The rain was lessening in intensity as Gaspar moved to speak to Mary. "Pardon, sir, I believe I know you, but am not certain. Are you not one of those who attended the birth of my son?"

"Good Mother, that you should speak to me at such a time. I am Gaspar."

"How wonderful that you should have been here at the beginning and the end!"

"Lady, I tried to stop--" Gaspar's attempt to speak ended in a sob.

As if she were his mother, Mary enfolded Gaspar in her arms and comforted the older man, "It was always to have happened in this way."

"I do not understand."

"It was foretold in the Scriptures and my Son spoke of it. Gaspar, your gift of frankincense, an offering worthy of my son's divinity, will be used when his body is anointed for final burial."

Chapter 6

It had been dark for several hours as Gaspar slowly approached the inn.   Reaching to unlatch the door handle, he was met by an excited Abram.   "You are safe!   We worried when sundown came and went, and still you had not returned.   Quickly, come!   We know of the crucifixion, but see what has occurred!"

Ushered forward, Gaspar beheld his old servant and friend seated at a table.   "Raheeb?" he incredulously questioned.

"My, Lord, I am well."

"How can this be?"

"At the height of the storm, when the thunder and lightning were at their greatest, I awakened and felt no pain.   I have been awaiting your return here for hours.   When you did not return, Abram and Judith invited me to eat the Seder with them."

"Raheeb, you have been very ill! You must return to your bed to rest!"

"My Lord, I feel no physical pain--only my great sorrow over the death of Jesus."

"Have you heard what else occurred during the storm?" Judith questioned.

Gaspar, still stunned by Raheeb's recovery as well as by the events of the horrifying day he had endured, could only look inquiringly at Judith who was clearly eager to speak. "The temple veil was torn right down the middle! A monstrous bolt of lightning struck it at the beginning of the storm."

Wonderingly, Gaspar responded, "I saw the lightning from Golgotha. I knew it hit in the city--but the temple--and to destroy the veil!"

"You were there at Golgotha?"

"On Calvary at the crucifixion?"

In concern, Judith halted the men's questions as she drew their attention to Gaspar's bloodied hand that she had just noticed. "How did you hurt yourself, my Lord? Let me cleanse it, and you can tell us of this tragic day."

Later, speaking to everyone, and not attempting to mask the heartache he felt, Gaspar began to relate the events of the long day. Pausing he said, "I tried all morning to stop it. I went to both Annas and Caiaphas, Pilate--twice. I even went to Herod--that weakling!"

"The son of the man who slew the babies?" Raheeb questioned, horrified.

"Yes, and clearly he has inherited his father's brutal ways. As we now know, it was he who ordered the beheading of the cousin of Jesus, John the Baptizer. Once in his presence, it took only moments for me to realize that he could be influenced through his pride. Although

I despised myself, I was momentarily effective in delaying the inevitable."

Judith inquired, "Why do you say the inevitable?"

"His Mother told me herself."

This time Raheeb eagerly spoke, "She is still alive! And Joseph?"

"I did not ask, but he was older than Mary as I recall--nearer our age. At the end as Jesus was being buried, his Mother noticed and remembered me."

"What a terrible day for a mother to endure!" Judith sympathized.

"It was dreadful. Her tears watered the earth."

At this point, Gaspar wasn't sure what to say in front of Judith and Abram, but they were obviously disturbed by the events of the day. Judith's next question indicated her continued interest, "Good Gaspar, you said earlier that his own mother told you it was inevitable that he was to die?"

"Perhaps I misunderstood her meaning. She seemed to be implying his death could not be stopped by any mortal."

"How could any mother know of her child's death--or any person know of another's? We all thought Raheeb would die any day, but here he sits saying he is well again!"

His own thoughts uncertain, Gaspar found himself at a loss for words. The abrupt interruption of two soldiers roughly opening the hostel door distracted them. "Innkeeper, bread and drink! Quickly, man, it's been hours since we ate! Have you seen anyone skulking in this neighborhood tonight? Soldiers sighted a member of a criminal gang in this area just past sundown."

"A criminal?" shrieked Judith.

"The two thieves hung on Calvary today--there was at least one more in the gang. We believe he's the half-brother of the leader Dismas. When we cornered them last week, Dismas could have escaped, but instead he took us all on and fought like a tiger. He blocked the door after ordering the brother to quit fighting and escape. We must have wounded the brother because we followed a trail of blood, but lost him somehow. The whole gang was wanted for crimes going back twenty years and more. They're wanted from here to Egypt."

After drinking half the tankard Abram had provided, the garrulous soldier continued, "He was seen on Golgotha at his brother's execution. As soon as we recognized him, we went after him, but he escaped in the dark and rain."

Judith pressed, "What does he look like? What was he wearing?"

The second soldier answered, "He blends in with everyone else in Palestine--brown hair, average height, somewhat darker clothing. He'll probably have a fresh wound, but we don't even know where it would be."

Gaspar quietly asked, "What will happen to him if he is caught?"

"Oh, we'll catch him all right! And if he's still alive after we get our hands on him, with all the trouble he's been to us, we'll put him up for show on Golgotha just like we did with the other two."

Draining the last drops from the tankards, the soldiers left, with the leader half-heartedly complaining to his comrade, "We'll be out chasing this thief all night, and tomorrow I've pulled guard duty at the tomb of the King of the Jews!"

Their crude laughter could be heard through the open window as they took up the hunt again. Striding away, his last words drifted back, "Tribune Sextus is in charge of the tomb and he never cuts us any slack."

Abram bolted the door after the soldiers left, "If a thief is around, we'd best take precautions." Guardedly he continued, "Free food and drink for protection--ah well. You do know why they're guarding your Jesus' tomb, don't you?"

As both men shook their head negatively and Gaspar encouraged him to go on, Abram answered while locking a window shutter, "The High Priests requested a special guard detail. They fear his followers will steal his body."

"Why would anyone do such a thing?" exclaimed Raheeb.

"There's a wild tale I heard from Isaac the tanner that Jesus said he would rise from the dead. Gives you the creeps, doesn't it?"

At the dumbfounded look of his listeners, he chuckled and continued, "The High Priests figure his followers will steal the body and then say he rose from the dead as he claimed he would. By asking the Romans to guard the tomb, the High Priests believe this will squelch any rumors and prevent it from happening altogether."

"Surely the Romans will not guard the body forever?"

"Actually, it is supposed to happen in three day's time."

Gaspar suddenly said in amazement, "You are right! Their Scriptures proclaim it and the high priests would definitely fear it! By plotting against Jesus and carrying out their cruelty, they may have created more problems for themselves than if he were alive."

"Are you saying you truly believe he will rise from the dead?" breathed Judith.

Pausing before answering, Gaspar answered thoughtfully, "I am not sure what I believe--I always knew he was to be someone special. For this reason Raheeb and I made the journey again here to Palestine to see if his destiny had been fulfilled. The heavens led us, and others from afar, to his birthplace in Bethlehem. Later, we three kings all had the same dream on the same night telling us to avoid Herod's treachery. He was surely protected then, and his birth happened as predicted of the Messiah. Stories are told throughout Palestine of his miracles. In our homeland we heard of him through caravan drivers. He cured the sick; expelled demons. I imagine you have heard that in Bethany, just miles from here, he is said to have raised a man named Lazarus from the dead."

"I believe!"

The confident words of Raheeb silenced the king and drew amazed gasps from Judith and Abram. "He will rise from the dead! I know it. My heart, which caused me so much pain and now does not, tells me it will be so."

"Think what you are saying," cautioned Abram.

Turning to Gaspar, Raheeb questioned, "When did Jesus die?"

"He was on the cross for hours."

"It stormed about three hours past midday. Did he die then?"

Quietly, Gaspar said, "It had been dark since mid-day with the threat of rain, but as soon as Jesus died, the skies above opened. At the very moment of his death, the storm struck with an intensity I have never experienced."

Raheeb spoke confidently, "How could you not believe that the wrath of an almighty being could cause such happenings, if one whom it held dear was being innocently punished? The heavens foretold his birth! The same heavens would surely storm at his death." Firmly he added, "I was healed today because of Jesus."

Abram muttered, "To say such things is blasphemy."

Staunchly, Raheeb eyed the landlord, "Abram, think about the temple being damaged in the storm."

"No, no, that was purest chance."

"Not everything can be laid to chance," Raheeb said, smiling gently. "It was not chance that led us to his birth. It was not chance that allowed the miracles to occur-- maybe one, maybe two, but not all. No mere magician in public places could fool thousands of people. The cures were performed on suffering people who in many cases had been stricken for years. Much of his life was predicted in the ancient testaments and writings. King Gaspar has studied them for years and often we have discussed the possible interpretations. Now, in our lifetime, those scriptures are fulfilled."

Lowering his eyes in humility, he ended, "We have been blessed."

Gaspar gently spoke to his friend, "Raheeb, your faith is inspiring. Would that I could share it entirely. But you were not present on Golgotha. He died in despair although earlier he forgave his tormentors as he hung in agony."

"Why do you say he despaired?"

"His last words ached with both physical and mental anguish. He cried out, 'My God, my God, why have you forsaken me?'"

Abram seized the words, "If his father was God, why did he call out to his God rather than to his father? No, Raheeb, this was not the Son of God, this was a man who had been disillusioned in life and even at the hour of his death could not face reality. He was just a man--not a god."

"Gaspar, were those his last words?" Raheeb entreated.

"Yes." Hesitating, he then added, "No, he did say something else. Let me think."

The two men waited expectantly hoping to hear words that supported each's separate stance. Finally, Gaspar admitted he hadn't heard the words clearly, but it seemed Jesus had said, "Into your hands I commend my spirit."

Raheeb's face lit up with joy. "He did not lose his faith!"

Abram graciously admitted, "While it would seem he did not lose his faith, I cannot believe that faith was well-founded. The Sanhedrin was wise to post a guard. If his followers have the same beliefs as you, Raheeb, he will rise by faith alone!"

Judith spoke out, "I have to admit a liking for the man. I never saw him or heard him--this inn and the cooking keeps me busy day and night. He certainly was no coward; he could have catered to the High Priests at any time. Even this morning--before his last words, a strong reprimand or maybe even the flogging would have satisfied them. He took on the moneylenders in the temple. Up against the High Priests--face to face. The nails in his hands and feet! I mean no disrespect for his sufferings and, truly, it is unbearable to think of them. To hang from his nailed hands for three hours! How could he endure it?

"His last words--well, I've cried out myself at times wondering if we have been forsaken. I imagine most of us at one time or another have felt deserted. He had more cause than some." She paused and sighed, "This has been a long, difficult day for all."

Abram slowly spoke, "I cannot name the reason why, but a sadness has come upon me. It is as if this day is the end of something. Jewish high priests and Romans united, the death of a personage you say the heavens drew you to--mayhap our world will never be the same again."

Holding out his hand to Raheeb, Abram continued, "It was good to share the Seder with you. Let us shake hands and remain friends always." Here he paused, then looking into the other's eyes, stated, "If he rises from the dead, your faith will be a lesson for us all."

"Time will tell," and Raheeb grasped the other's outstretched hand in friendship.

The next day was the Sabbath and the Jewish community obeyed the law of Moses as it was written: "This is what the Lord has commanded to be done. On six days work may be done, but the seventh day shall be sacred to you as the Sabbath of complete rest to the Lord. Anyone who does work on that day shall be put to death. You shall not even light a fire in any of your dwellings on the Sabbath day."

Strict laws regulated activities including the amount of walking which might be done. In conquering Palestine, the Romans were forced almost of necessity to adhere to the same slow Sabbath regimen; therefore, the day was generally one of rest for everyone in Jerusalem. This particular Sabbath, being a part of the Passover festivities as well as the day after the death of one whom many now remembered as being ever of gentle heart, seemed to take an eternity to pass.

Not wanting to offend their host, Gaspar and Raheeb abided by the edict to limit walking although they longed to go to the gravesite. Gaspar confided in Raheeb all that he had seen and said and been saddened by during the previous day. The wounds were too new, too painful for them to think beyond the present. To wonder what the days to come would bring was to speculate about a new order, a new world. Each preferred to let it reside in the future and so they talked mainly of the yesterdays in their life.

Some of their conversation concerned the young criminal still on the loose. Raheeb speculated the reason for his being seen in the neighborhood, "Could he have followed you?"

"It is possible. However, I lost sight of him almost as soon as we had climbed the hill. He became angered when I expressed sympathy to him; I would say he would not seek my company."

"He is a thief, my Lord. We must take particular care. Your robes would have indicated to a professional thief that you are a man of some wealth. For such a man, it would be easy enough for him to discover your whereabouts."

"The soldiers apparently spotted him on Golgotha and immediately pursued him. I, of course, stayed until the end--until Jesus died, and remained to honor him at his entombment. The brother would have been in hiding long before I returned unless he was a fool, and he certainly didn't seem one in the short time I spent with him."

"Well, we would be extremely foolish ourselves not to take extra precautions."

"Surely, he would leave Jerusalem since the authorities are after him still."

"The gates are being especially well guarded. He won't be able to escape easily. I learned from Abram, who always has the latest news, that in addition to trying to capture the escaped thief, they are hoping to round up the followers of Jesus."

"For what reason?" Gaspar asked.

"I think it would only be to question them. Probably the Romans want to frighten them--I don't think they could be kept in prison."

"Hopefully, you are right, Raheeb. I believe they are mostly fishermen from up north around the Sea of Galilee. The Romans will discourage any attempt to idolize Jesus. The Jews, too, won't want Jesus turned into a martyr. Both the Romans and Jews would probably be satisfied to warn the men to disband and to return to their nets in Galilee."

The conversation edging too near the future, they dropped the topic and pursued another. And so they passed the Sabbath. Rejoicing over Raheeb's recovery, they chose not to probe too deeply into its timing. Significantly, they made no plans for the future although their fixed purpose in returning to Palestine had been to find Jesus.

Chapter 7

On the morning after the Sabbath, Raheeb awoke while darkness still reigned and was thrilled to realize that he did not fear the day. It was a pleasure to breathe deeply and not to be concerned that he would overtax himself in doing so. Since his lingering illness the previous year, he'd not had the strength of his youth or even middle years. During the last months, he had somehow managed to hide his weakness from Gaspar, and thus had been able to accompany his King back to Palestine. Gaspar, of course, knew he was not completely well and this had been the main reason Zaphta each day had gone ahead to secure lodgings and prepare the way for the two older travelers.

What would this day bring? If the Scriptures and Jesus, the Christ, were to be believed, it would be the most glorious day ever. Today, a man would rise from the dead. Had he really been present to see the Son of God as an infant? To have held this child of destiny in his arms! Raheeb wondered when they would learn of the actual event. Perhaps it had happened already! He arose, dressed and went downstairs. Others in the hostel still slept so he went out to the street where the sunrise was bathing the dawn in a half-halo of gold.

A movement at the side of the inn caught his attention. Someone was over in a storage area beside the building. "Who is there?" he challenged.

Although no one replied, Raheeb felt certain someone was nearby. Knowing he should be more cautious, he strode over to the side of the building where the noise had occurred. Investigating thoroughly, he could find no one. His thoughts turned to the thief known to be in the neighborhood. He had the feeling that the man had slept in the lean-to and his own early rising had startled the sleeper. What would he be doing lurking here? Given what little Gaspar had learned of the man and of his crucified brother, Dismas, Raheeb wondered if he should fear for his King's safety. Intuitively, though, he felt there was another reason than theft that the man was still in the area.

Dismissing the gang member from his mind, Raheeb considered what to do now. If Gaspar awoke and found him not there, he would be concerned. But it seemed ridiculous to wake him to say, "Go back to sleep, I'm going to the gravesite. By the way, the thief might be near." Deciding it was still so early yet that he wouldn't be missed, Raheeb turned west to where Gaspar had told him the grave was located.

Approaching the Gate of Ephraim in the northwestern sector of the city, a commotion drew his attention. Raheeb wondered who would be creating such a disturbance this early in the morning. Intent on seeking the tomb, he hoped he would not be kept from continuing his quest.

As if his own thoughts had forecast the scenario, Raheeb abruptly halted as soldiers dragged forward a young man who was struggling to escape. Two soldiers roughly clasped him, and Raheeb wondered at the panic in their voices.

"He's a thief!"

"This is your last crime for sure!"

"No, you're wrong! I spent the night in the city!" the young man shouted in vain.

"Shut up, or we'll shut you up permanently!"

"Someone took the body, and you're a known thief."

The grizzled veteran growled, "You'll be hanging from a crossbar tomorrow."

The words about someone taking a body, compelled Raheeb to intervene. Even as he spoke, he wondered at his own actions. "What are you doing with my servant?" he demanded.

All eyes stared at him in varying degrees of surprise including those of his supposed servant. Hoping to keep the soldiers off-guard, Raheeb knew that an authoritative tone would most impress them, "Unhand him, I say."

Seeming to ignore the soldiers, he then addressed the man he felt was surely a thief. "Young fool, running ahead of me. I should let these soldiers have your carcass, the little respect you show to me and to our King, Gaspar."

The mention of a king further unnerved the soldiers, but their natural Roman arrogance and training quickly reestablished itself. The leader angrily stated, "Your servant strangely resembles a thief we've been chasing for days!"

"Well, you will have to keep looking," he said firmly. "King Gaspar would be quite offended if you were to arrest one of his people."

Eyeing the captive's unkempt look, the soldier snorted in derision at this remark, but now seemed less confident. One of the other soldiers spoke up, "We're wasting time here. The body snatchers are getting away as we stand here arguing."

Raheeb couldn't help but ask, "What body snatchers?"

Throwing a threatening look at his comrade, the first soldier said, "Grave diggers were looting this morning. Take your man. But be prepared to answer questions later about this affair. It's too early in the morning for honest people to be about!"

Although anxious to question the gravedigger remark and to learn more why the soldiers seemed so obviously panicked, Raheeb thought it best to leave immediately. He would now be subject to arrest himself if the soldiers found out he had duped them.

"Stay close this time," he harshly spoke to the released captive knowing the soldiers were still listening.

"Yes, master," the other responded still dumbfounded at his luck.

Rapidly putting distance between themselves and the soldiers, neither man spoke. Raheeb knew the youth was preparing to bolt as soon as he could. Without looking at the other, he ordered, "Don't be a fool, there are soldiers everywhere."

"Why did you do it?" the other asked with no trace of gratitude.

"Do you know who I am?"

"You are the other old man's servant."

This confirmed for Raheeb that this was the thief who had helped Gaspar up Golgatha. "Why have you been hanging around my master? Do you seek to rob him?"

The youth threw him a murderous look, and angrily responded, "If I planned to rob him, it would have been done already."

"You will rue the day you harm my king."

"Do you think two old men scare me?"

"Does a cross on Golgotha and an ending like your brother's scare you?"

Satisfied that this effectively had impressed his brash companion, Raheeb sought the information he really wanted. "What was the talk about a body being stolen?"

"By all the gods, how would I know? All I care about at the moment is food." Noting Raheeb's stern look, he continued, "I ran into those soldiers while trying to avoid three others. They're certainly in an uproar about something, that's for sure."

Raheeb looked upward and confidently stated, "He has arisen!"

Wondering at the sanity of the man beside him, the other edged slightly away, but considered it in his best interest to follow along for the time being.

Each wrapped in his own thoughts, they approached the inn in silence. Pausing before entering, Raheeb cautioned, "I warn you again, harm no one in this place. I will seek counsel with King Gaspar as to what becomes of you."

"No man decides my fate!"

"If you choose to leave, do not plan to sleep again where you did last night."

Startled and infuriated again, the younger man could find no words to respond as Raheeb opened the door and entered. With no better prospects and at least momentary safety along with the possibility of food, he reluctantly chose to follow.

Their entrance into the inn was met by several pairs of inquiring eyes. Gaspar, Abram, and Judith were in the common room, and Raheeb wondered what to say and where to begin.

Gaspar took the initiative after recognizing the brother of the criminal Dismas. Not wanting to alarm Abram and his wife that a thief was in their midst he greeted, "Raheeb, who is your young friend?"

Having hoped to speak in private with Gaspar, and with no experience in fabricating the truth, Raheeb brought forth as honest a tale as he could, "I was out earlier and met this young man. After walking together, I asked him to break his fast here. I have brought you a customer, Abram."

The landlord looked askance at this opportunity and considered offering a bath rather than a meal to the disheveled newcomer. A customer was a customer, however, and if Raheeb vouched for him, he supposed it would be all right though he doubted if his establishment was safe with this man inside. "Welcome, we have fresh fruit and new-made bread."

Gaspar intently asked, "What is your name, young man?"

Knowing that the old king had recognized him, he answered sullenly, "Daniel."

Judith's take on the whole matter was apparent with her next remark, "There is a known thief in the neighborhood. Raheeb, you were not wise to be walking alone so early."

Raheeb could wait no longer, "Sire, Abram, Judith, I have news. Jesus has risen!"

His words were greeted by degrees of incredulity.

"How can you know this?"

"What did you say?"

"Tell us what you have learned."

In his excitement, Raheeb forgot his efforts to shield Daniel, "Arising early, I decided to try to find Jesus' burial place since this would be the third day in the tomb. When I arrived near the gates, soldiers had arrested Daniel here because they were seeking grave robbers."

Ignoring the remark about Daniel, Abram interrupted, "There is no proof in that!"

"I know it was Jesus whose body was missing!" Raheeb said excitedly.

Gaspar questioned, "How can you be sure? Did they say his name?"

"No, I think they didn't want me to know the real story. But what other likely explanation could there be for the soldiers' panic? They spoke of a grave theft and were arresting Daniel."

Gaspar quietly addressed Daniel, "You were there first, please tell me what happened."

Daniel, who had been eating as soon as Judith placed the food in front of him, swallowed a large mouthful and plainly preferred to take another bite of the loaf of bread clenched in his hand rather than to answer questions. All his life he had survived by his wits—half-truths or outright lies; now was no different, "I know nothing except that the soldiers were looking for a scapegoat, and found me alone."

"They didn't tell you why you were being arrested?" Gaspar asked.

"Raheeb told you already."

"Did they mention the name of Jesus?"

Gaspar noted the instant pain in Daniel's eyes as the name apparently resurrected bitter memories of his brother dying with Jesus. Daniel looked down quickly, and as if the food in his mouth had turned to stone, muttered, "No."

Raheeb spoke, "The soldiers were shouting of someone taking a body. Grave looters don't take bodies; they take gold and other valuables. Soldiers on the day after the Sabbath aren't out in numbers nor are they panicked about grave robbers." He continued confidently, "Jesus' body was not in the tomb which the Roman soldiers had been assigned to guard. Jesus has arisen as he said. I believe it with all my heart."

His obvious faith drew Daniel to let down his guard and say hopefully, "This Jesus died with my brother."

Judith, aghast at these words, shrieked, "I knew it! A thief at my table!"

"Silence, woman, we all know this," Abram commanded, though he had the grace to look sheepish at the exasperated look his wife threw him.

Gaspar intervened, "Dear Judith, please pardon this improper use of your establishment. Let us try to sort out what problems we might have brought you and decide on a course of action."

Judith sank into a nearby chair that King Gaspar drew out for her. After a moment's pause, she moaned, "We'll all be arrested!"

Raheeb felt he had to make a clean breast of his part in this matter. "She might be right. I told them this man here was our servant, though they seemed to recognize him as part of Dismas' gang."

"Our gang was three people only and two died on Calvary."

Abram looked at his royal guest, "They will come to question Raheeb."

Gaspar instantly responded to the unspoken plea of his host, "We will depart immediately, and you must say you know nothing of our plans."

Judith became an efficient force at this point, "Abram, go to my brother, he will find means of travel and help get them through the gates. Raheeb, why are you still sitting? Go--pack for your journey! Gaspar, we must move quickly. You, there," she eyed Daniel who had started to rise, "do not move from where you sit!"

Each man instantly obeyed her commands and by mid-morning, the travelers were approaching the Water Gate of the city that was manned by three intent Roman soldiers. Gaspar and Raheeb exchanged worried looks as they slowed their camels.

"Halt!"

Raheeb responded, "King Gaspar and his two servants leave today for the Orient."

"No one leaves the city this day except by signed decree from the Governor."

"My good man, why?"

"I don't question orders, I just enforce them. Without papers, you won't leave."

"We could easily have obtained papers, but did not know of this requirement. Our business is urgent."

Arrogantly disregarding Raheeb, the guard impatiently demanded, "Why is that man's face covered? Show your face, now, or suffer Roman justice for your cowardice!"

Daniel, face and hands covered with linens, did not move. Raheeb urged his camel forward to quietly address the guards, "My companion is garbed such as he is so your eyes will not be offended. He has contracted the vilest of diseases--leprosy--while we have stayed in this miserable climate. Accept this offering, please, to use as you see fit to cleanse you or your city of his rotting flesh." Holding forth a bag weighted by coins he shook it encouragingly.

Wanting the offered largesse, the soldier still knew his duty. "First, he will have to show his face and speak." Rudely, he added, "We're seeking a dead man, and he qualifies it seems."

"His tongue has rotted, but your soldiers can undo the wrappings on his face. He has lost fingers, but can still ride with the reins wrapped around what is left of his hands."

"Raise your arms to show you still live," the guard ordered.

The specter slowly lifted hands and arms around which the reins were indeed wrapped. The camel snorted angrily when the reins tightened whether by accident or design no one could have known. As the animal viciously kicked out, the body swayed dangerously. None of the soldiers relished the task of looking beneath the wrappings. The coins were another story, however. Grabbing the hefty bag, the soldier curtly ordered, "Begone—before he falls off!"

As the travelers urged their mounts through the gates of Jerusalem, one of the soldiers spoke for all, "Dead men rising from the grave! Dead men riding camels! What's in that bag won't do any of us any good."

Chapter 8

Wearily, the travelers halted the camels and prepared for the awkward moment of dismount. This was their tenth day of hard riding to put as many miles as possible between themselves and danger. Each evening the two old men had collapsed with fatigue at the evening campsite. Daniel had most unwillingly tended the animals and done the heavier camp duties. Their fatigue left little desire for conversation except for brief directional comments. Theirs was an uneasy alliance, but all were interdependent upon one another.

Daniel was not in the least happy with the situation. Granted the two old men had helped him escape, but as soon as he felt safe enough and had what he wanted from Gaspar, he planned to disappear. He could have traveled faster alone, but the safety represented by the King's power and money was not to be disregarded.

Gaspar and Raheeb had left Jerusalem without having satisfactorily fulfilled their mission and now were subject to arrest if Daniel's disguise was penetrated and his identity became known. To have had to flee from justice in the company of a thief on the day when Jesus was to have proven himself to be the Son of God was bitter to both men.

Raheeb was totally dismayed to have placed his King in harm's way. Gaspar felt responsible for Raheeb since it had been his idea to return to Palestine in the first place. Their aching bones continuously reminding them they were no longer young, they depended more on Daniel as each hour passed. It was Daniel who decided where to pitch camp each night. It was also Daniel who tethered the animals and it was he who put out the simple food that Judith had shared so liberally with them.

Raheeb seemed particularly weary this evening, but Daniel had decided that tonight would be his last with them. He was familiar with this area and knew there were caves in the surrounding hills that had harbored his brother and him in the past. It was a place well known to others who lived on the shady side of the law and who would be perfect company for Daniel.

He noticed Gaspar looking at him and wondered if his uneasiness and plans to abandon them were apparent. Not being one who had spent a lot of time considering others in his lifetime, he still knew it would be wrong to abandon the old men, particularly in this area of known ne'er-do-wells. Tonight, however, he was determined to succeed against Gaspar in what had turned into a quest for him.

In an effort to begin a conversation, Daniel inquired of Gaspar, "How does your hand feel?"

"If we didn't have to ride each day, it would have healed quicker, I'm sure. Your leg seems healed."

"It was never much. A few more days ride north and east out of these hills and you'll be safely on the road taking you to Baghdad."

Gaspar leveled a look at Daniel and gently corrected, "Yes, we will all be safe then."

Daniel was struck again at the acuity displayed by the old King. He always seemed to be a step ahead of Daniel and to know what Daniel was thinking even before he himself knew he was thinking it. For a person who made his living by outwitting others this was a peculiar position to find himself in day after day. He had even come to feel that the reason Gaspar went to bed so early each night was not just because he was exhausted, but also because it allowed him to avoid conversation.

As if to again disconcert Daniel, Gaspar began to talk, "You seem to know this area well, Daniel."

His natural instinct for self-preservation as usual coating his answer, Daniel replied, "It's been years since I passed this way."

"This area reminds me of the hill-country around Bethlehem with its caves."

"Yes, there are some in the area."

"A good place for such as we to rest in safety."

The irony of his phrasing was not lost on Daniel who was beginning to enjoy the evening's sparring. "Safer for some than others."

Raheeb who was resting nearby smiled at the exchange, but had no desire to join in the verbal battle.

Gaspar asked, "Do you think it would be safe for you to abandon your disguise now that we have ridden so far from Jerusalem?"

"It would probably be safe, but I'll keep it close in my robes in case a Roman patrol appears."

Gaspar questioned, "Would it be safe to assume that we are not being followed after so many days with no pursuit?"

"The closer you are to your kingdom, the safer you will be. Rome has a long arm. It would not do to disregard it. Keep moving and you will be safe."

Gaspar decided to challenge their young companion, "Your words this evening seem to indicate the possibility that you are considering traveling alone."

"My way is not yours."

"Why must this be so?"

"Our paths go different ways."

Gently Gaspar spoke, "Your brother's death could free you from those old ways."

Daniel shrugged while answering, "In our land there is an old saying, 'Once a thief, always a thief.'"

"Would your brother Dismas want you to die as he and your other comrade did?"

Rising abruptly, Daniel angrily trod away into the night, "Leave it alone, old man!"

"How long did you stay with your brother that day?" Gaspar called out.

The words stopped Daniel in his tracks and he wheeled toward Gaspar snarling his rage, "I stayed long enough to see him dying with your Jesus. Three criminals--one no better than the others."

"I did not mean what you think I meant, Daniel," Gaspar said soothingly.

Refusing to be appeased, Daniel shouted and gestured wildly, "You don't know what I'm thinking or feeling or anything about me. My brother knew I was there for him, and that I would have sacrificed my life for him as he did for me."

"I was not faulting you for leaving, Daniel. Your brother knew you loved him, I'm sure."

"You haven't any idea what kind of a man he was. He--"

Daniel's emotions became too much for him, but he didn't charge into the night as he had before. Dropping to his knees, his shoulders slumped forward, and he hung his head.

"He--allowed you to escape while he fought the soldiers."

Attempting to stop the tears staining his cheeks, Daniel tightly closed his eyes. Trying to banish the scene that he had relived constantly since his brother's capture, he ground out, "I should have stayed and helped him. I was a coward. I ran--I let him be captured and he died to save me."

"You were injured. You would both have died then. He wanted you to live."

Daniel stared blankly until Gaspar explained, "Soldiers eating at Abram's inn told us some of the details."

Haltingly, Daniel uneasily confided, "I had to see him one more time. I had to be there. It was the hardest thing I've ever done knowing what I'd see. I couldn't stay long-- there were too few people and too many soldiers."

"Do you want me to tell you what happened?" Gaspar offered. "Is that why you followed me and have stayed with us?"

Daniel roughly responded, "I know what happened-- he died miserably."

"Then what do you want from me?"

"He said something--I was too far away. Maybe-- maybe you heard and might remember."

87

"I heard. I remember."

"Tell me."

"If I tell you, it will change you. It is nothing you might think he would have said." Quietly, he added, "He did not speak of you."

Dejection apparent in every line of his body, Daniel seemed to seek further pain, "I must know. I have--had no one else."

"Do you know anything of the third person crucified that day?"

"Do not start about him again! My brother is the important one to me!"

"He became important to your brother it seems."

Gaspar waited for any further reaction from Daniel. When none came, and Daniel's eyes remained downcast, the King told of the words exchanged between Jesus and Dismas. After telling Daniel how Dismas had rebuked the third man, Gaspar ended, "Your brother came to believe in Jesus. His words carried deep conviction as he asked Jesus to remember him when he came into his kingdom. Jesus promised him more than remembrance, however. He proclaimed that both he and your brother would be that very day in paradise."

Raheeb and Gaspar expected some immediate response, but none came. Daniel seemed to be made of stone until at last his shoulders heaved mightily as the two men respected his silence.

Gaspar moved to give whatever consolation he might, but as he came near, Daniel startled him by harshly snarling, "No! I want none of your religious sympathy. Your Jesus caused the death of my brother!"

Raheeb cried out, "Daniel! How can you say such a thing?"

Violently, Daniel rose and shouted, "He would not have been on the cross if this Jesus had not filled his head with hope and lies."

Angrily, he glared at Gaspar and Raheeb, "My brother was bewitched by your Jesus. Near the River Jordan, we had--a place where it was safe for us. A religious fanatic named John began to speak nearby and crowds came to hear him. It was entertainment to see the people in their white robes being baptized. We used to while away the time joking about them in the heat of the day. Always he spoke of another who would come after him and whom the people should follow. Dismas started to change. I told him he was a fool.

"I know now that we were in Jerusalem because Dismas was following Jesus. We would come across crowds in different towns where Jesus was--I thought we were trying to get rich off the crowd! Dismas would disappear and then return later. I know he was going out to hear the crazy talk of this religious nut just like he had listened to John."

Daniel ranted on, "That is why he let me escape--he had become soft!"

Raheeb had struggled to his feet and now went to Daniel, "You are wrong. They were not lies, Daniel. Jesus promised those who believe in him everlasting life."

"Who would want such a thing? Another life like this one?"

"No, a life of good deeds on earth, then the reward in the next."

"I never want to hear the name of Jesus. I curse him and you and all that he said and ever will say. Rising from the dead! What a trick—what a joke! My brother is dead! Do you hear me? Dead--because he listened to a crazy man!"

89

Raheeb seemed to be searching for words to appease Daniel when suddenly he lurched forward and slowly sank to the ground in obvious pain. Gaspar reached him first although Daniel was closer.

"Raheeb, is this like before?"

Mutely, the older man nodded and closed his eyes as another wave of pain shot through him.

"Daniel, help!" Gaspar pleaded.

Chapter 9

In two weeks, much had changed. Summer's heat was upon the land. Gaspar had now begun to worry if Raheeb would make it home again. Daniel had reluctantly helped them find shelter in a cave where he had stayed in the past. He had clearly violated an unwritten code in bringing the two men to the isolated area where men on the other side of the law regularly sheltered.

Gaspar had expected Daniel to abandon them once he had learned what his brother had said from the cross. With Raheeb stricken again, the youth had stayed on, although clearly his desire was to leave. As they sat in the coolness of twilight on this evening, Gaspar asked him why he had stayed. Daniel succinctly answered, "Twice you have helped me when you could have as easily let me fend for myself. Raheeb saved me when the soldiers had me under arrest. I pay my debts."

Daniel suddenly stopped speaking and strained to see in the faint light. Gaspar, alerted by Daniel placing his fingers to his lips ordering silence, waited in some alarm. Out of the darkness, a voice called, "Can anyone hear me? I've lost my way--is anyone here?"

Deciding the voice was more alarmed than alarming, Gaspar ignored Daniel's hiss for further silence and called out, "Here, friend. Come, join us."

"Peace to you. My thanks for your welcome."

The newcomer relieved his listeners by his mild greeting and pacific demeanor. Their visitor had a luxuriant head of pure white hair and a beard equally as white. His clothes were simple and he carried nothing but a walking staff.

"Sit here," Gaspar welcomed. "Daniel, please bring the water gourd to refresh our fellow traveler."

His history betraying him, Daniel questioned, "Where do you hail from that you carry no water or other provisions? We're a long way from anywhere."

"What need is there to worry when people like you befriend me daily. I need no extra coat or clothing. Possessions would only slow me."

"What is your name?" inquired Gaspar.

"I am called Levi or Matthew, whichever you choose."

Trenchantly, Daniel asked, "Why two names?"

"Formerly I was a tax collector and was known as Levi by most who knew me. My new friends call me Matthew."

Before Daniel could again insult the traveler, Gaspar spoke, "Well, we are new friends and shall call you Matthew. I am Gaspar and this is Daniel. Our comrade Raheeb is resting over there."

"Again, my thanks. I was afraid I had become lost and had not followed the directions given to me."

Daniel eyed both Gaspar and Matthew mutinously as he returned to his interrogation, "Where are you bound?"

Calmly Matthew answered, "After this stop, I am on my way to Galilee."

"You are certainly lost if it is Galilee you seek."

"I have a good friend who I believe may be in this area. I decided to come here first because of the good news I bring him, although you are right, it is out of my way."

"Tomorrow you can be on your way." Daniel's tone conveyed his meaning.

"Daniel, Matthew is welcome to rest here in our camp as long as he cares to do so. Possibly you can help him find his friend when he is ready to resume his journey."

Matthew looked at Gaspar almost in wonder, "Since you have welcomed me as you have, I gladly accept your offer. Blessings to you, Gaspar."

Tentatively, Matthew continued, directing his words more to Gaspar than to Daniel, "Perhaps you might be interested in the good news I have brought?"

Daniel chose to interject, "By the gods, why would we be interested in news you have brought for someone else?"

Matthew deliberately chose his words, "My commission is for all men of good will."

Daniel looked confused at Matthew's response. Gaspar looked intently at the newcomer before he carefully replied, "We would welcome the news. Have you been in Jerusalem?"

"I have been in Jerusalem for over a month. Having been directed to go to Galilee, I felt the need to inform an old acquaintance of the great events which have recently occurred there."

Daniel sneered, "This would be a friend who called you Levi?"

Unruffled, Matthew answered, "Yes, you are right, Daniel."

"You do know that the people in this area are cutthroats, thieves and other assorted ruffians?"

"Is that what you are?"

"Daniel, cease plaguing our guest. Matthew, do share the news with us. To what great events do you refer?"

Matthew suddenly seemed unsure of himself and of what to say.

Daniel shook his head in disgust, but Gaspar continued undeterred, "Is your news from Jerusalem concerning events around the time of the Passover?"

"Were you there then?"

"I witnessed a crucifixion."

"You were on Calvary?"

As Gaspar nodded, Matthew could not look him in the face, "We were--I should have been there, but I was afraid--we all were."

"I knew him longer than you did," Gaspar replied gently.

Matthew leaned forward asking eagerly, "How could this be?"

"Do you know the story of his birth?"

"No, but how could you know it, if I don't?"

"I was there."

Incredulously, Matthew and Daniel stared at the old man. Gaspar said, "Raheeb was there too. We followed the stars to his birthplace at Bethlehem in Galilee of Judea.

Two other kings from eastern countries also read the signs in the heavens. In our wonder at the phenomena in the skies, we sought further enlightenment and knowledge. For months we each individually had followed the celestial omens. Eventually, we found one another. The star led us to a humble cave where Jesus, his mother Mary, and Joseph were sheltered--much as we are here tonight. But enough of the distant past, tell us your news."

Again Matthew hesitated although it was obvious that at least Gaspar and Raheeb yearned to hear they knew not what. Raheeb finally requested baldly, "Did Jesus rise from the dead?"

"Yes, he arose."

"You--you have seen him?" Raheeb implored.

"I have both seen and spoken to him."

"My God," Raheeb breathed in awe.

"Impossible!" Daniel roared out.

Gaspar urged, "Tell us everything."

"I caution you that the chief priests and elders refuse to acknowledge that Jesus rose. They say it is impossible, as Daniel obviously believes. They accuse us of stealing his body. We are the chief suspects, along with others who knew him. Even the Zealots, the fighting faction of the Jews, are suspected. The Romans haven't yet realized what this miracle means. They are strictly concerned with keeping the peace."

Matthew continued, "As I told you, he rose from the dead. It was on the third day of his death after the Sabbath at dawn. Mary Magdalene, one whom Jesus saved from herself, and other women were bringing perfumed oils to properly anoint the body for burial. They and the Roman soldiers found the huge stone rolled back. After the soldiers ran to report the theft, a man in dazzling snow-white garments addressed the women saying, 'Do not be frightened. I know you are looking for Jesus the crucified, but he is not here. He has been raised exactly as he promised. Come and see the place where he was laid. Then go quickly and tell his disciples.'

"Overjoyed, yet fearful too, the women hurried to carry the same good news I have just shared with you. He honored Mary Magdalene by appearing to her first. The other apostles and I had gathered together in fear in the same room where we had celebrated our last meal together with Jesus. We found Mary's story difficult to believe, but only Peter and John had the courage to run to the tomb.

"Since he arose from the dead, he has appeared to many of us. He greets us with words of peace just as I greeted you tonight. The first time he appeared he showed us the wounds in his hands and his side." Matthew paused at the memory.

Before continuing, he looked toward Gaspar and Raheeb then finally at Daniel, "He gave us a commission, 'As the Father has sent me, so I send you.'"

"What did he mean?" urged Gaspar.

"We are to spread his teachings. As he did while on earth, we preach forgiveness of sins, love of neighbor, and good deeds."

"You said he has come to you several times?"

"Yes, on the first occasion my good friend Thomas was not present. You have to know Thomas to appreciate what happened. He has a reputation for having to see things with his own eyes before believing. Anyway, after we told him Jesus had come while he was out shopping for food, he would not accept our story. He said he would never believe without probing the nail prints in Jesus' hands and without putting his own hand into Jesus' side.

We were shocked that Thomas would say such a thing about The Master's wounds.

"About a week later, despite locked doors, Jesus came again. 'Peace be with you,' he said. Then he told Thomas: 'Take your finger and examine my hands. Put your hand into my side. Do not persist in your unbelief, but believe!'

"Then Thomas exclaimed, 'My Lord and my God!' Jesus said to him words I know I'll never forget, 'You became a believer because you saw me. Blest are they who have not seen and have believed.'"

Gaspar and Raheeb spoke almost in unison, "I believe."

Daniel said nothing, but it was apparent that Matthew's words had made an impression on him. He queried, "All the others believed, including you?"

"Well, the first time, I admit some of us thought he might be a ghost. That was when he calmed us by offering, 'Touch me, and see that a ghost does not have flesh and bones as I do.' Joyfully we shared our meal of fish with him. Later we talked that a ghost would not have need of food."

Daniel tried to convey disinterest, "What did you mean that he teaches forgiveness?"

Considering carefully before speaking, Matthew finally responded to Daniel's question, "Let me tell you the story of how I first met Jesus. One day, back when I was known as Levi--" Matthew paused to smile at Daniel, "I was sitting outside the Customs House collecting taxes for Herod Antipas. Jesus walked past and said, 'Follow me.' I could not help myself, and so I left my work and followed him to hear his words.

"In his honor that evening, I held a reception in my house. I invited many friends and acquaintances. The

Pharisees and their scribes were horrified and complained, 'Why do you eat and drink with tax collectors and sinners?' Jesus replied, 'It is not those who are well who need the doctor, but the sick. I have not come to call the virtuous, but sinners to repentance.' He then told them to go and learn that he desired mercy, not sacrifice."

Matthew again directed his words to the youth, "Daniel, after his resurrection, Jesus spoke to us and opened our minds to a new understanding. As the Messiah--the savior of the world--he suffered and died for our sins. My sins....your sins....the sins of all peoples since the time of Abraham and Isaac....since the beginning of time. His death upon the cross--the son of man and the son of God--opened the gates of heaven. Sincere sorrow for sins, penance, and then the remission of sins--we are to teach and to baptize those from all nations who choose to follow his way."

Gaspar eagerly spoke, "Matthew, will you come to my country and teach my son and my people about Jesus and his words of healing, forgiveness and mercy?"

The Apostle responded without hesitation, "I will, Gaspar. I will come."

Through the night, Matthew, Raheeb and Gaspar exchanged stories about Jesus. Matthew told of the three years of public life, while Gaspar and Raheeb spoke of Jesus' birth, and the writings Gaspar had studied. Matthew absorbed the details and in discussing Herod the Great's motives, he told them of his own encounters with Herod's son Antipas for whom the taxes were collected and then delegated. "I became a tax collector because I could read and write and use the abacus. I was well paid, but became ostracized because of my job and relationship with Herod. Jesus did not shun me. He loved me for what I was.

"Gaspar, I will tell your people that Jesus lived as he taught. He told us to obey the Laws of Moses, but also that the two greatest commandments were even above these. First, he said we are to love God, his father, with our whole being. Second, we are to love our neighbor as ourself. During the years I spent with him, he taught of a loving God. He reviled no people except hypocrites and those who follow the laws so closely that they do not love their neighbors. I saw him lose his temper only once, and that was in the temple when he chastised the moneylenders."

As the stars shone through on a gloriously clear night, Daniel listened to words that promised salvation. He looked at the three men and considered how unlike they were, yet each was united in a faith that the promised Messiah had been in their presence. They talked openly of cures and events the likes of which the earth had never seen. In his heart a small but distinct part of him wanted to accept this offer of a new world and a new way of life, but his own entrenched experience to have faith and trust only in himself and his brother were too engrained.

When Daniel finally prepared to sleep, he expected to toss and turn, to dream erratically of angels and spirits walking on water. Instead, his dreams were sweet remembrances of his older brother Dismas and his childhood, and he lay wrapped in sleep well past the dawn. He awoke to find Matthew and Gaspar talking again and wondered if they had done so all night. It surprised him to feel disappointed that he might have missed something important.

Gaspar finally noticed that Daniel was awake and greeted him, "Good morning. Matthew has decided he must be on his way. He lingered to say farewell to you."

Matthew approached and warmly embraced Daniel who, feeling awkward, shrugged free quickly. Taking no offense, the kind-hearted man took his leave of Daniel, "We will meet again when I fulfill my promise to Gaspar."

Reacting churlishly at this assumption, Daniel answered, "No. You will not see me. I'm only with these two for a few days more."

Matthew ignored his answer, instead responding, "Peace to you, Daniel." Turning to Gaspar and Raheeb, he bade them farewell.

Individually, he addressed King Gaspar, "You have the right of it, I should record the events of Jesus' life." Matthew raised his arm in a gesture of farewell and strode out of sight.

Chapter 10

After Matthew's departure, it had been decided that if Daniel could find one or two men to help with chores and assist in conveying Raheeb on a portable bed of sorts, they would slowly continue their journey. They had traveled in this way for three days more trying to keep the ill man as comfortable as possible. The previous evening the men had demanded their pay and this morning, not too surprisingly, the three travelers had awakened to find themselves alone. They had determined to continue, but now at mid-day with little progress, found themselves on the edge of a large flock of sheep.

Shepherds in the distance were tending the animals. Rather than travel wide around the flock or cut through the center scattering the sheep, the travelers decided to call it a day and to make camp in this area of clear and sparkling waters. The frisking lambs provided amusement for the weary Raheeb and he declared pleasantly, "How wonderful to live this way. I could remain here forever."

They became aware of anxious bleating in the hills to their left and laughed that one of the lambs had wandered too far. The calls became distant and Raheeb worried aloud that it would become lost. He urged Daniel to go after it, but the younger man said, "A lost sheep is not my concern. It wouldn't come to me anyway. It would be too scared and would only run farther."

Raheeb noticed one of the shepherds moving toward the hills. Somehow he had become aware that one of those in his care had wandered. Watching the man until he was out of sight, Raheeb told Daniel, "Don't worry, one of the shepherds knows what has happened."

Daniel jested, with his newfound humor, "I'll stop getting ready to look."

Several hours later, while the flock had meandered south of them, the same shepherd appeared in the distance. He moved toward their camp and they noticed a young lamb nestled in his arms.

Gaspar called a welcome, "Please join us for a while. Take some refreshment."

As he entered the clearing, the shepherd soothed the young animal with a graceful gesture. Calmly he spoke to them, "My thanks for your invitation. Peace to each of you."

Without any self-consciousness, he moved toward Raheeb first. Extending his hand, he placed it on Raheeb's arm so that he would cease trying to rise. "May my lamb rest with you?"

"Will he stay?"

"He brings my special peace to you, my friend."

Raheeb settled back on his pallet and momentarily pondered the strange answer. His eyes remained riveted on the shepherd and Daniel wondered why the man's beauty and gracious words appeared to now leave the sick man awe-struck.

Daniel handed the shepherd a cup of water and in doing so noticed that the man's beauty was marred by fresh scars on his hands. In accepting the cup, the stranger briefly locked eyes with Daniel as if acknowledging a special bond between them.

As he turned from Daniel, he went toward Gaspar who had intended to speak. Instead, the shepherd addressed him, "You have traveled far, but your reward will be great." Again the words seemed to have a deeper meaning, and Gaspar wondered that the man could seem to know him.

The shepherd sat on an elevated rock and drank deeply from the cup Daniel had given him. No one seemed inclined to break the silence although there was no awkwardness in the situation. The man exuded an indescribable presence that was nevertheless calming.

Daniel broke the stillness, "Your friends and flock have moved on."

"We are old friends, they can find me if there is need."

They seemed puzzled by his words and he questioned them, "'What is your thought on this? A man owns a hundred sheep and one of them wanders away. Will he not leave the ninety-nine out on the hills and go in search of the stray? If he succeeds in finding it, believe me, he is happier about this one than about the ninety-nine that did not wander away. Just so, it is no part of your heavenly Father's plan that a single one of these little ones shall ever come to grief.'"

While telling this story, the shepherd had seemed particularly to be addressing Daniel, although it was Gaspar who answered. "Yes, you are right. As a ruler,

I know that when I have brought happiness or justice to one of my people who was disheartened or who needed my help, that it gave me greater happiness than helping those who needed less."

The shepherd addressed him, "Wise, Gaspar."

The old king knew his name had not been told to the newcomer. He peered closer and recognition dawned on him in a spiritual awakening. Smiling gently, the other requested, "Have you any bread and wine that we might sup together?"

While noting, but not understanding Gaspar's stunned look, Daniel responded that they had some left. He brought what little they had and apologized for the small amount.

"There will be plenty for all."

While the man took charge of the preparations, Daniel was surprised to note the broad smiles being exchanged by Raheeb and Gaspar.

Somehow it seemed appropriate that the shepherd should bless the meal and then share it. Extending his hands over the bread and wine, he looked toward each of the men. "Do this in remembrance of me."

Rising, he approached Raheeb first. Holding out first the bread and then the cup of wine, he quietly spoke to Raheeb. Gaspar heard his final words and briefly closed his eyes, "Your pain will cease tonight, my faithful Raheeb."

To Daniel he spoke only briefly, "You will labor long, my friend, but your work will be rewarded in heaven." He extended the bread and wine toward Daniel who reached for both, not taking his eyes from the shepherd's face.

Turning to Gaspar, the spiritual personage smiled deeply, "As you came to me in the beginning and are here now, ever shall you be with me in a world without end."

At his words of limitless possibilities, their eyes closed to consider his message. When they looked again, he was no longer in the camp.

Postscript

A King's Story has been a work of love for me. When I wondered at my temerity in writing such a book, became anxious over details, or worried about writer's block, again and again I felt the presence of God. Whether I was riding in my car or sitting in church, I begged for signs of spiritual support, and after a while peacefully waited for them to occur as I knew they would.

To be specific let me share the first such occurrence. After coming up with the initial plot, I had decided that for research purposes, I would need a *Bible* and maybe even a book like *The Robe* (which I had never read) to be able to flip from page to page, take notes from, and just generally use for research. Obviously the family *Bible* was not one of the books to use. Within four hours on this same day, both books were mine. When I arrived at the school where I worked, a note was in each teacher's mailbox that books would be available for the taking due to the library's end-of-the-year closure of old or unused books. At mid-day when I entered the library, I walked straight to the center table of discarded books and side-by-side, lay both an old paperback *Bible* and *The Robe.*

My book is grounded in research by scholars before me, and also in the words of the evangelists. Exact words from passages of the Bible were frequently used. A major resource was the voluminous text *The Birth of the Messiah* by Raymond E. Brown, S.S. This book was recommended to me by Bill Shea, a parent of one of my older son's friends, and also at that time a professor at Saint Louis University. In Brown's book I found a brief statement that the Holy Family was apparently robbed while staying in Egypt; portions of the plot thus fell into place, and can be read about in the Prologue of my book.

My then sixteen-year-old son, Bret, through his education at the St. Louis Priory, was my compadre on research, my helpful gopher and initial proofreader. I would say, for instance, "Now I need the name of the well in the Jerusalem temple." Within moments he usually had the requested information and frequently it was from one of the Bibles I was using—yes, the family Bible was eventually used for study purposes—the most it had ever been used! Bret was invaluable chatting to me about details of the men and women who lived 2,000 years ago. A special thanks is due to Bret's teachers who imparted so much of their knowledge to him. My thanks also to Bret for his perceptive words when he read the last chapter.

So that there will be no sibling rivalry, I am grateful also to my younger son, Nick, who was in primary school when I originally wrote this book, and who supported me, hugged me, and made more than one meal for himself. I am certain that his months of cooperation came from his heart rather than my statement that we were going to Disneyworld after the book was completed.

I am grateful to all my family for their encouragement and especially to my Mother, another excellent proofreader, and to my older sister, Philipa, who gave me pertinent background about Matthew the Evangelist for whom she had named her beloved son. This leads me to share with you another of those special mystical moments I experienced in the writing of *A King's Story.*

At our school picnic, before I knew enough about the Bible to know that only in Matthew's Gospel can be found the story of the Magi, I told her that in honor of her stillborn child, Matthew, that I was going to use the Evangelist Matthew to be the person who tells Gaspar, Raheeb and Daniel about the events of Easter morning. She told me she was fairly certain that Matthew had gone to the lands of the Magi to do his work and that he had died there.

Who invited Matthew to come to the lands around present day Persia? Was it actually King Gaspar himself? Why is the story of the three kings found only in the Gospel of Matthew? Could it have been Gaspar who encouraged Matthew to write his Gospel?

With the above questions in mind, can it be doubted that at least one of the three Magi would have wanted to have known what became of the baby boy whom the star of Bethlehem had led them to decades earlier? Logically, the youngest would have been most able to live another thirty-three years, and be energetic enough to travel. Having Gaspar return to Jerusalem during what is now known as Passion Week gave me the nucleus for *A King's Story.* Gaspar and Raheeb, together with Daniel, the young gang member, and the hard-working Judith and Abram, represent all peoples whom the Christ was born to inspire--high born, low born; Christian, non-Christian; male, female; scholar, scamp. In the opening chapters, the caravan drivers, the Greeks, Edomites and other wayfarers along with Sahran, the Jewish/Aramaic trader, carry this same message that the Good News is for all people in all places.

Creating Daniel, the fictional ne'er-do-well brother of Dismas, the Good Thief, provided a young man to assist Gaspar when Raheeb became ill and also reintroduced the theme that Jesus died for all men. The Good Shepherd of the last chapter who is visiting the shepherds of Christmas Eve is concerned not only for the flock, but will go to any length to save the lost sheep, i.e. Daniel.

As for the title, I leave it up to you, the readers, to decide who the King may be.

My hope is that *A King's Story* will help spread the message that the Good News is for all times, as well, including the exciting days of the newest millennium. Men and women of good will hopefully celebrate the past, and look to the future, as the world continues to strive to live the words of the humble man born at Bethlehem who desired all peoples to love his Father and their neighbor as themselves.

A King's Story -
Chapter Synopsis

separately hear stories of a "Master" who fed thousands from a few fish and loaves of bread, and a semi-humorous tale of a magician said to have brought a man back to life in the city of Bethany. The travelers are unwittingly in the surging Palm Sunday procession before Passover.

Chapter III - Believing their search for Jesus may end at the great Temple of Jerusalem, the two old men arrive to find it has been desecrated by the Galilean himself. At the words of Jeroboam, the High Priest who proclaims the Rabbi Jesus has now lost all credibility, Raheeb suffers a heart attack. Young acolytes assigned to assist the ill man energetically discuss a heated verbal confrontation between Jesus and the High Priests. Comments by one about an "Uncle Mark" refer to the future Gospel writer.

Chapter IV - King Gaspar learns of Jesus' arrest at Gethsemane on the Mt. of Olives. Attempting to use his royal influence to assist Jesus, Gaspar seeks out Caiaphas, Pontius Pilate, and King Herod. Gaspar flatters Herod, trying to save Jesus' life. Gaspar slyly comments, "For a man who is said to be a king, he certainly doesn't play the part well."

Chapter V - Unsuccessful in his efforts to save Jesus, Gaspar staggers toward Golgotha after being hurt himself on a thorn bush. A young thief named Daniel self-servingly bargains to help Gaspar climb the heights to the crucifixion site. Trying to outwit Roman soldiers by being with the old man (and thus getting up to Calvary safely), Daniel eventually admits to Gaspar that he is the brother of Dismas, one of the two thieves being crucified with Jesus. Gaspar witnesses the death of Jesus and sees him placed in the tomb.

Chapter VI   Soldiers, having spotted the young gang member Daniel in the neighborhood where Gaspar is staying, stop for refreshment, and one grumbles, "We'll be out chasing this thief all night, and tomorrow I've pulled guard duty at the tomb of the 'King of the Jews'!" Abram, landlord of the inn, and his wife Judith, discuss religion and life with Gaspar and Raheeb. The words spoken and issues raised reflect the possibility that people of all faiths can live together peacefully.

Chapter VII - Raheeb, apparently having been healed at the hour of Jesus' death, rises early on Sunday to visit the gravesite. Approaching the Gate of Ephraim, a commotion draws his attention as soldiers sight the thief Daniel whom they've been seeking for three days. Raheeb unaccountably befriends the criminal saying the young man is King Gaspar's servant and had merely run ahead. The words to the Roman soldier, together with bringing the thief back to the inn, will inevitably cause problems for Abram and Judith. Through a ruse Gaspar and Raheeb are able to smuggle Daniel through the now well-guarded gates of Jerusalem.

Chapter VIII- Days later Daniel remains furious over his brother Dismas' death that occurred as a result of trying to save Daniel himself. The younger brother admits he was following Gaspar hoping to learn his brother's last words spoken from the cross that he was unable to hear because the soldiers had spied him and given chase. Through a series of prior events, Daniel believes Jesus totally responsible for his brother's death. Harshly, he curses Jesus. In attempting to pacify Daniel, Raheeb suffers apparently a third heart attack.

Chapter IX - Grudgingly, Daniel stays to pay his debt to Gaspar and Raheeb. Three weeks pass, when a stranger comes to their campsite. Calling himself, Matthew or Levi, he says he has greetings for men of good will. Daniel fights his every word, but Gaspar and Raheeb realize he brings word of Jesus. Matthew wonderingly learns of their presence at Jesus' birth. In turn he tells them he has seen the risen Jesus. The words, as Daniel is slowly being converted, come from the Gospel of Matthew. (Note:

Matthew was the only Evangelist to write of the Magi's visit.)

Chapter X - Shepherds in the distance tend a large flock of sheep that is blocking the weary travelers' way. Deciding to camp, they see a frisking lamb which becomes separated from the flock. One of the shepherds follows the lamb. Later, the Shepherd comes to their campsite with the rescued sheep. Through his words of peace, his counsel to Daniel of a good shepherd searching for a lost sheep, and his other actions including breaking bread and sharing wine with them, Raheeb first, and then Gaspar, recognize Jesus.